Husbands Who Won't Lead

&

Wives Who Won't Follow

Husbands Who Won't Lead & Wives Who Won't Follow

JAMES WALKER

BETHANY HOUSE PUBLISHERS
MINNEAPOLIS, MINNESOTA 55438

Published by Bethany House Publishers
11400 Hampshire Avenue South
Bloomington, Minnesota 55438
www.bethanyhouse.com

Bethany House Publishers is a division of
Baker Publishing Group, Grand Rapids, Michigan.

Printed in the United States of America

ISBN 0–7642–2350–X

The Library of Congress has cataloged the 1989 edition as
follows:

Walker, James.
    Husbands who won't lead and wives who won't follow /
James Walker.
      p. cm.

    1. Marriage—Religious aspects—Christianity. I. Title.
BV835.W35   1989
248.8'4—dc19   89–20
ISBN 1–55661–009–2   CIP

To my Father, who taught me how to be a husband, to Joyce, who still teaches me to appreciate it, and to Nate, who showed me how to love the process.

JAMES WALKER is currently a free-lance writer and practicing psychologist in Colorado Springs, Colorado. He received an M.Div. from Talbot Theological Seminary with an emphasis in practical theology and counseling and a Master's in Community Psychology from The University of Northern Colorado. He has been a pastor with the Evangelical Free Church. He and his wife have three children.

Contents

I met my husband at a dance. Now, years later, it seems as if I'm still dancing in the dark with a total stranger. I would like to turn on the lights and look at this man, or just sit down and rest, but I can't. So I just keep moving, pretending I'm having a good time and waiting for him to talk to me. I guess I'll just keep dancing until I die.

—A wife who wrote anonymously

1

Dancing in the Dark

Many a woman today lives the same hollow, lonely life of the one who wrote this letter. Bearing a constant ache in her soul, she determines to hang on, but without hope that her husband will change. She is convinced he will never take the lead in their marriage or with their children—much less develop emotional intimacy with her. She may have lost touch with what it really means to be a woman. Worse, she may even be resolved never again to be vulnerable to a man because she cannot bear the constant pain of disappointment.

Consequently, she may decide to "fight fire with fire." She may put on an attitude that conveys: "If you refuse to take the lead in my life—if you cannot or will not meet my needs and those of our children—then I will manage on my own." And this conclusion is certainly affirmed in modern society. "Be independent and self-sufficient" is the rallying cry for today's woman.

And what about today's man? He "has it all together" in his power suit and tie, and he disappears each morning into a very different world than the one he shares at home with his family. Responsible and usually effective in his workaday environment, he returns to his other world of home at a time when he would just as soon drift away while he tunes in the latest ball game.

The truth of the matter is, today's man has found his role radically redefined from that of his father or grandfather. It is difficult for men today to even understand the uniqueness of their God-given position in the family. Traditional masculinity—which admittedly has included some cultural baggage—also incorporated the view that the father was the chief role model, embodying integrity, loyalty and self-sacrifice. Masculinity has been reduced to ridiculous "macho" images that breeze across our TV screens in beer commercials or "tough-guy-cop" movies. Today's "man" can get away with using women, avoiding children, and never being chained by commitments or emotional attachments. The other media image presents a somewhat wimpy, soft-headed father who doesn't quite know what's going on but who contributes witty, offbeat comments on everything.

So whether today's "ideal" man is a muscular shell who is ruthless on the field of competition and in business or an interested but fuzzy-headed bystander in his family's life, the man's role at home is neither defined nor understood. Without a clearly articulated and lived out role model of manhood, society is left with a caricature of media fantasy.

With both men and women trying to prove that they are tough enough to make it alone, is it any wonder that, for so many, marriage is little more than "sparring"—or, in the silence that surrounds each confrontation, a cause for loneliness and despair?

For others, the time pressures and distractions of modern life have eroded the energy, attention, and patience that are vital to sustaining a healthy marriage and family.

Can husbands and wives stop the cycle of tension, find an answer to the sense of loneliness, abandonment, lack of direction? I believe they can. Marriage is still one of God's greatest gifts to His children. And it is His plan for marriage—maybe "antiquated" to sophisticated moderns—that holds the blueprint for rebuilding unity, mutual trust, and the potential to mirror His relationship with His Bride, the Church.

Where do we find this blueprint? Not surprisingly, God has inscribed some of His own plan for strong marriage relationships in the very nature and character of men and women. Besides the obvious physical differences, there are basic mental and emotional contrasts—with many variations between—that may or may not be visible. Going back to the Genesis account, Adam was created one way; Eve was created in another. With different strengths and weaknesses, resources, and needs, man and woman were built to fit together. And though it is God who is the ultimate answer to the deepest needs of every human, nonetheless He created male and female: Man was made to lead, provide and protect; woman was made to respond, nurture, and provide the moral influence of the society.

As I noted at the outset, our modern "view" of the roles of men and women has changed radically. But the plain fact is, the basic characteristics and built-in sexual differences between men and women have never changed. So my question is: With so many marriages on a collision course with destruction, how can we afford to hold on to new-found attitudes of independence and emotional detachment?

The God who created us gives us the best instructions on how to relate to one another.

God's Blueprint in You and Me

In Genesis 2, God fashions a man. In our Lord's own estimation, "it is not good for the man to be alone" (Gen. 2:18). It was Adam's solitary condition that prompted God to "make a helper suitable for him."

To many women today, the term "helper" is thought to be demeaning. How can someone be a "helper" and be an equal in function and value? As the word is used by God, it has an exalted quality. It does not imply that the helper is merely an assistant to someone who is otherwise competent. It means someone who enables a person otherwise incapable. Far from being a term for a second-class citizen, the word is used by God even in reference to himself.

In Ps. 70:5, David cries out, "I am afflicted and needy; hasten to me, O God! You are my *help* and my deliverer; O Lord, do not delay." And Jesus referred to the Holy Spirit of God as "the Helper" (John 14:16, Amplified).

If the role of helper is a legitimate one for the Creator of the universe, the One who holds everything together, then it is hardly a lesser role or a demeaning term to refer to a woman in partnership with a man as his helper.

When our Lord planned a partner for man, He calculated the best way to make one who would be *suitable*. His infinite wisdom saw something in the nature of man that could find no satisfaction without a female counterpart. That deep longing in the maleness of Adam could be quenched and brought to its fulfillment only in Eve. Likewise with Eve; in her relationship with Adam before sin entered the world, she had no problem with respecting him. The thought that she was less than his equal never entered her head. There was nothing to prove. She could be comfortably female and allow Adam to be contentedly male.

In fact, her contentment seems to have been caught up in the bold concept expressed in the word *suitable* (Gen. 2:20). What does it mean to be suitable? Does it mean to be stepped on and ordered around? Does it mean that the roles of a husband and wife are interchangeable, depending on what the need is and on the abilities of each partner?

We need to examine this matter of sex differences and sexual roles more carefully in order to approach those questions.

At the Heart of It All

Deep within each man and woman is a common longing: the desire to find comfort, companionship, and fulfillment. God installed this longing in us for a purpose. One of the purposes of marriage for a man is to become as truly masculine as he can be. Likewise, a woman's fulfillment in marriage comes as she becomes as distinctively feminine as she can be. Each will have a unique role and definable function. God has so designed marriage that a husband will meet his wife's spiritual, emotional, and physical needs, and vice versa. Outside of marriage, God has other methods to bring people to full potential as male and female.

The blueprint God has in mind for a marriage is a coupling of two distinct designs, one male and one female. To deny the uniqueness of the sexes and supplant God's sexual ground rules with a misguided struggle to swap roles or deny their existence altogether has serious consequences.

A Male World and a Female World

A husband and wife can work at identical jobs, but often they will hold dissimilar views of life, and may seek completely different sets of emotional rewards. In their courtship they may have been fascinated by these differences. In marriage, however, those same characteristics can be viewed as a threat. When friction occurs, differences are easily mislabeled not for what they are, but simply as a lack of love.

To understand our mate we must first understand his or her sexuality. There are unique differences that are revealed by even a casual observation of the male and female anatomy. In Chapter 3 we'll take a closer look at some of the more subtle distinctives between men and women. Without being too graphic or improper, we see suggestions in God's design of the male and female body that point to deeper conclusions about who we are as people.

(Note: None of the following is intended to be absolute for every individual. These are generalities and trends that have largely remained changeless over time, despite the current myths of a unisex society.)

First, we see in the strength of the male body God's plan for him to be the protector. It is he who also initially gives life as he assumes the initiative in the relationship with a woman. Throughout recorded history, society has depended on male protection and what men by their strength provide. In the short span of the last hundred years, we have taken away a man's hunting rifle and put him at a computer—which may have obscured but not removed him from the role of protector.

Second, we know that the responsibility of managing the earth's resources did not begin as a result of the Fall. It was part of God's original and highest ideal for Adam and his sons.

In Gen. 2:15 we are told:

> Then the Lord God took the man and put him into the garden of Eden, to cultivate it and to keep it.

The responsibility for cultivation of the earth points out a man's bent to be the one who provides for his family's needs. This is not just a role he plays and *therefore* he is masculine; it is the very nature of his masculinity that drives him to seek his greatest satisfaction and respect by performing the function of provider.*

Third, a woman is made physically, emotionally, and spiritually for the central task of nurturing. Trying to make males and females interchangeable in the family structure is a contributing factor to the family's loss of leadership. This is not an issue of fathers changing diapers but the far deeper questions of a father's view of himself and how that fits with his wife's and children's perspectives. Conversely, how does she view herself in the family?

Fourth, it is part of the feminine nature to be a receiver and a responder. One of the great pressures placed on women today is the notion that it is not all right to be feminine in this way. The "new and improved" model of femininity is aggressive, self-reliant, rock-solid emotionally. The attempt to live up to this legend causes some women to deny their basic inner nature, which is that of a responder.

This does not mean that a man cannot respond, or that a woman should never take leadership. It only means that the depths of a man's sexuality are affirmed when he is allowed to lead. Likewise, the innermost yearnings of a woman's nature are touched when she responds to her husband's leadership. To deny this is to deny nature.

Two Halves—One Great Big Hole?

We can resist the notion of sex difference (which to modern men and women seems obsolete) and try to argue it away. Don't we all know women gifted in business, men who love to

---

*There is a natural resistance to the idea that anatomy determines destiny. Many have tried to demonstrate the illusion of female-directed families where the male assumes a nurturing role in housekeeping and child care, while the wife by virtue of her giftedness and special abilities goes off into the world to earn the family's income. I am aware that the attempt to succeed at it just brings frustration. Our sexuality is not determined by the roles we play in society, but those same roles are greatly influenced by our sexuality.

nurture and rear their children? But the sex differences will not disappear, regardless of how strenuously some will try to argue against them.

By ignoring the fundamental sex differences of a mate, many couples find their marriages riddled with cracks that widen into huge gaps in their relationship. Though a woman may appear strong (perhaps because her husband has never met her deep need for protective tenderness), she can become deeply unhappy or even chronically depressed without knowing why. A man may appear to enjoy the benefits of his wife's higher-paying job, yet underneath, without his even knowing why, there may exist a spirit of competition, evidenced by cutting remarks and more demands placed upon his wife than she can humanly handle. The effects upon her can be fatigue or a near collapse emotionally.

Somehow, for many couples today, it feels as if there is a great big hole in the middle of their relationship. Granted, there are many possible explanations why these huge gaps open up. But one of the biggest reasons must surely be that husbands and wives fail to recognize the underlying sexual differences that motivate their spouse.

Maleness and femaleness were not created by God in order to drive couples apart; there are two halves to a marital whole. They can be fully understood and appreciated only when they are in the presence of each other.

In 1 Cor. 11:11–12, the Apostle Paul writes:

> In the Lord, neither is woman independent of man, nor is man independent of woman. For as the woman originates from the man, so also the man *has his birth* through the woman; and all things originate from God.

Each sex carries with it the ingredients that will stir the other up to its greatest potential and highest goals. Neither should be independent of the other. Nor should we try to blend each into a nonsexual, interchangeable personality.

Coupling—Or Collision?

A marriage is intended to be a coupling of these two sexualities. It is God's design that a couple become attached to each other, and in so doing they can help each other grow into whole, mature people.

Many times, however, marriage is not a coupling but a collision of sexualities. At the opening of this chapter, we read a letter from a woman describing the emptiness of her marriage and we looked at examples of the way men and women approach marriage differently. Our sexual contrasts come up in virtually every conversation. When we are not meshing, not attached to each other in a positive, building, strengthening way, our sexual differences will begin to grind, to wear us down and even, eventually, to destroy personality.

A couple we'll call James and Darla recently gave me a blow-by-blow description of their relationship. Though they were at odds, they were attached to each other all right, but it was an attachment of frustration, not love. Darla desperately wanted James to be the leader—so much that she began to assert herself and her demands on him. By the time I saw them, their marriage was very nearly destroyed. Listen to the way each of them describes what was going on:

> Darla: I love James and need to know that he's there. But when he comes home and I don't get the attention I want or the help I need, I make sure he knows about it. At times I really pour it on. You know, the real guilt trip! I say things like, "You know you should be the leader in the home. So how come I have to make all the decisions? Why do I always have to wear the pants around this family? I'm always praying with the kids, giving them the discipline, and being dad and mom all the time. I give the kids excuses for you but they know . . ." and stuff like that.
>
> I know those anger jags never work. And when I finish I'll feel rotten. But I just can't help myself and I think I need to get it out of my system.

I asked James, whose eyes were firmly fixed on his shoelaces, what Darla's temper tantrums did to his thinking.

> James: She's right. When she finishes I know she's right. I think of myself as a total failure. I want to do her and the kids a big favor and just disappear. In fact, I'm even worse than what she says. I feel sorry for her,

'cause I don't think I can ever change. But I sure don't want to lose her. I know she's my only chance. No other woman in the world would put up with what she puts up with.

James and Darla were attached to each other. Neither thought they could survive without the other, yet they were making each other absolutely miserable. The more they saw their own existence and their own self-worth reflected in the behavior and words of their mates, the more they believed the image and the more resigned they became to living with it.

One of the first things men and women must do, if they want to get free from this destructive kind of attachment and move into a relationship that is fruitful and building, is to *stop* using their mate as a mirror of their own performance and self-worth. There are two actions we can take that bring equally bad results. The first is to resist, pull away, and rebel from your spouse's attempts to pressure you into fitting an image; the second is to give in to the pressure and conform.

You may be saying, "Hold on a minute! If I'm not supposed to resist or conform—then what's left? What am I supposed to do if I want to become the truly masculine man, or the truly feminine woman God wants me to be? How do I become a healthy, whole person who knows how to rightly relate to my spouse?"

The answer requires your full attention and commitment. You must stop measuring your worth as a man or woman by the reflection you see of yourself in the eyes of your spouse. And you must definitely stop trying to judge your sexuality and your worth against the standards of the world. *Both will reflect distorted images of you, because they are imperfect mirrors.* And if you think that a distorted image is the right one, you will twist and misshape yourself trying to fit into a mold that is filled with flaws.

The only "mirror" that will accurately reflect who you were created to be—man or woman—is the unchanging Word of the God who created you. God's standard is the only perfect reflection of redeemed sexuality and a redeemed, healthy union between male and female. Far from being outdated, God's standard continues to hold up against the world's false standards today, images that are destroying men and women and marriages and scarring untold children who see home only as a place where one sex is out to put down and destroy the other.

The solution to conflicts in your marriage, then, is not to "keep your options open," looking for an easy out—it is to press deeper into God's plan, which is to discover the true roles of man and wife in a beautifully ordered marriage.

Does this sound impossible to you? Or too difficult to work for? I assure you, it's not an impossible goal. God can reorder your marriage. He can help you overcome criticism, hostility, disappointment, emptiness.

And His starting point is most often our own hearts. Seldom does He change the circumstances before He changes us. When we find a battle going on in our marriage, the first place we should look for a solution is where our Lord starts—our own heart. And when the changes begin, husbands and wives will see that they don't need to spend the rest of their lives as strangers dancing in the dark.

Power is of two kinds. One is obtained by the fear of punishment and the other by the art of love. Power based on love is a thousand times more effective and permanent than the one derived by the fear of punishment.

—Mohandas Gandhi

2

Who's in Charge Here? — The Battle for Control

Control, and who has it, is the ultimate, unspoken question in a marriage conflict. And when the issue is decided, neither side enjoys the result. Even if one spouse achieves maximum influence over the other, the victory is bittersweet.

For instance, if a wife allows her husband to dominate her, he comes to dislike her for being much less than a whole person. She is not his companion, nor his helper, nor his friend. She is simply his tool. Conversely, a wife who succeeds in gaining total influence over her husband will find herself living with a man she cannot respect. She can never be sure he loves her or just wants to minimize conflict. To win at the battle for control is, finally, to lose.

For many people, control is something they will go to any lengths to maintain, no matter how painful or how destructive to the emotional well-being of their spouse. Normally, we think that the person who treats his or her spouse in this way is suffering from a skewed idea of love. In fact, if the domination is severe enough, they may actually be suffering from another malady—"person addiction"—an idealized notion of how a relationship is supposed to function. They cling to one person who, they believe, gives them significance. The effect is an unhealthy pattern of relating in spite of pain.

Howard Halpern writes this in his book *How to Break Your Addiction to a Person*:

> When someone is your Attached Fetish Person, it is easy to distort who he is in a way that plays up his good points and diminishes or obscures his bad points. That can be an innocuous or somewhat helpful distortion that can serve to grease the wheels of the relationship over the inevitable rough spots. But when you idealize traits that are causing you much difficulty, or if your idealization is blinding you to ways the relationship is harmful, then this idealization becomes a malignant self-delusion.[1]

Halpern goes on to discuss the relationship of a couple in which the worst aspects of a mate were viewed as his positive strengths. The husband maintained a rocklike independence and a curious inability to express tenderness and emotion. The wife began to look at the problem as a matter of her own "immaturity" and saw her husband's inability to be loving as one of his greatest strengths as a man. This illusion trapped her into a life in which her own need to be loved and esteemed by her partner made her feel weak and caused her to lose self-respect, a no-win situation!

It is often this sense—that we must become *better*, or that we are the only one who can "take" what a mate dishes out—that traps us in a controlling relationship. But it is also, oddly enough, a trap for the controller. Again, a man who must be in charge is attracted by a woman who feels insecure and has a great desire to be cared for and protected. This is an unhealthy mix.

In his book *The Inner Male*, Herb Goldberg talks about this destructive selection process.

[1]Howard Halpern, *How to Break Your Addiction to a Person* (New York, N.Y.: Bantam Books, 1983), 101–102.

As a result of this powerful need to control, [a man may marry] the feminine woman, with whom he feels initially comfortable, because she accommodates him out of fear and manipulates or "uses" him in order to get what she needs. She doesn't put pressure on him to get personally involved or to "open up" in a way that will expose his deeper feelings because she is as afraid of them as he is, her protestations about wanting intimacy notwithstanding. Unconsciously, she gives him dominance by *reacting* to him rather that *acting*, giving up her power and self to him even though eventually and inevitably this builds rage and even hatred of him in her. Unconsciously her feminine internalization means she will fear and resist taking overt and direct control and power. She has as much anxiety over taking this control and power as he does over losing it. Because of these mutually reinforcing defenses, they initially feel attracted to each other.[2]

There are two prevailing patterns among people in the death grip of control. We may call them "The Smothered Woman" and "The Missing Man."

The Smothered Woman

The "smothered" woman is one who is married to a man with the compulsive need to be in charge. She lives an uncomfortable, "invisible" life and always feels she is unnecessary. Her husband may need her work, appreciate her ability to handle the children and be gratified by the sexual release she provides him, but her ideas—her needs, her wants and her soul—may seem uncared-for and ignored.

This woman may, in fact, have become totally dependent. She has never needed to learn to operate the remote control on a TV set. That device is always found in her husband's hand. She would never think of shifting the dial on the radio and will just as likely freeze before she changes the controls on the electric blanket or the car heater.

---

[2]Herb Goldberg, *The Inner Male* (New York, N.Y.: NAL Penguin Inc., 1987), 125–126.

Domination—even under the guise of "spiritual leader-ship"—carries with it the smear of inequality. It leaves the man or woman with a feeling of helpless abandonment. This is the opposite of what Christ intended:

> For all of you who were baptized into Christ have clothed yourselves with Christ. There is neither Jew nor Greek, there is neither slave nor free man, there is nei-ther male nor female; for you are all one in Christ. (Gal. 3:27–28)

Leadership does not mean domination. The entire idea that one sex is mandated by Scripture to dominate the other is foreign to God's thinking. Unfortunately, we have gotten our idea of leadership from worldly and carnal examples. We hold up the local football coach or corporate magnate as exemplary models of what it means to be a leader. Jesus contrasts His view of leadership with ours:

> You know that the rulers of the gentiles lord it over them, and their great men exercise authority over them. *It is not so among you*, but whoever wishes to become great among you shall be your servant, and whoever wishes to become first among you shall be your slave; just as the son of man did not come to be served, but to serve, and to give his life a ransom for many. (Matt. 20:25–28)

The picture of leadership Jesus intended to leave in the Christian is that of Him stooping over the feet of all the dis-ciples (including Judas) to wash their feet. (See John 13:4–14.) Peter may have had this portrait in mind when he wrote to church *leaders*:

> . . . not as domineering over those in your charge but proving yourselves models for the flock to imitate. (1 Pet. 5:3, Williams NT)

If a husband is to assume the biblical role of leadership in the home, it will be the leadership that is mandated to us by the example of Christ and the instructions of Scripture, not by *Who's Who in America*. Men who habitually dominate their wives, however, rarely do so because they misunderstand the

Bible. These are men who feel most comfortable emotionally when they have absolute control over the women around them. They are frightened by women, although they would never admit it. The real root of their behavioral problem lies in their thought patterns. This man cannot lead as Christ intended until he roots out his habit of intimidation and the false idea of what it is to be "a man."

The Insecure Male

The other portrait of the controlling male is the man who dominates because he is terribly insecure. This man is usually transfixed by the image of his father. Quite often he lived in a female-dominated home, where his own father was missing or distant. Others have endured a smothering or hostile mother who directed everything. It is the nightmare memory of this home-life that causes him to dominate his adult home, with a need for absolute male control. To accept less is to risk the possibility of living out his father's dominated life, something he cannot bear even to think about. He may deeply love and sympathize with his dad, but he cannot respect him. To allow his wife to make a decision that will impact him is to live with the possibility that his worst nightmare is coming true, that he has become a man like his father, a man not deserving respect.

The Pressure to Perform

For many men, to be male is to be always "on stage." These men assume it is always their "move," their time to do something and their responsibility when anything goes wrong. They seldom see themselves as being pursued by a woman. They assume the active role, and constantly feel the pressure to live up to those expectations of performance, self-inflicted or otherwise.

In *Men and Marriage* (an excellent study on the differences between men and women), George Gilder writes about the need of men to do something to prove their manhood. This masculine need is expressed in many different forms around the world, depending on each nation's culture and history. He contrasts that phenomena with a woman whose sexual identity is a matter of the biological clock she carries around within her:

> At an early age he is, in a sense, set at large. Before he can return to a woman, he must assert his manhood in action. The Zulu warrior had to kill a man, the Mandan youth had to endure torture, the Irish peasant had to build a house, the American man must find a job. This is the classic myth and the mundane reality of masculinity.[3]

Men are goal-oriented. For some men, marriage is just another something on his resume—an important goal to be sure, but still a goal and not a relationship. Part of his goal in marriage is to be in control, to have no problems, or, in lieu of that, to deny problems. There is an uneasy pressure to perform—to be responsible and accountable—inherent in being male.

Masculine Confusion

A little girl is rewarded for her beauty and charm; but as a little boy grows to be a man, he finds out that his position in life depends upon the "big three": status, power, and money—all of which come as a result of his performance. With the extreme confusion in our society over the place of masculinity, it is unavoidable that some men are drawn to the popular stereotypes. So they measure themselves by their status, power, or wealth.

The Danger Signals

While the following list is by no means complete, it represents some of the major masculine identity problems resulting in the need for control to a greater or lesser extent.

---

[3]George Gilder, *Men and Marriage* (Gretna, La.: Pelican Publishing, 1986), 8.

Any problem is his problem.

Some controlling men feel a compulsion toward assuming a parental role for their wives. Like Professor Henry Higgins in the musical *My Fair Lady*, they assume the woman they live with is a product of their creation. Ed and Sharon (not their real names) related the story of one of the many frustrations of their ten-year marriage. Sharon called it a "communication problem."

"Whenever I tell Ed that I'm tired and need a day off," she began, "he takes it personally. No matter what my problem is, he seems to believe he should talk me out of it. So I get sermons, pep talks, and even temper tantrums from him. It's best that I say nothing."

Ed responded by saying, "I feel responsible for what happens to her. You know, it's my spiritual duty as her husband. If there's a problem, then it's up to me to do something about it."

In further conversation we discovered that this type of smothering behavior showed itself in Ed's advice on her housework, what she should fix for dinner and when it should be ready, and even what Sharon should wear on various days—all unsolicited of course. Sharon could not think of one decision she made regularly that affected the whole family.

If a man is dominating his wife, she might even express pain and find that she is a threat to his ego. The slightest twinge of an emotional problem acts as a finger, pointing at his poor leadership and an indictment of his lack of wisdom.

Ideas and favors must be his idea.

Sharon clasped her hands tightly. Then quietly, deliberately she said, "I feel that every time he opens a window, it's a breeze and—and every time I open it, it's a draft. I still remember being in our first apartment the day after our honeymoon ended. I cooked a nice dinner, then afterward he went to the television and left me alone with the dishes.

"I told him nicely how I would love to have his help and just be able to talk to him while I worked in the kitchen. He got angry and told me, 'I'd love to serve you, but when you *demand* it, it takes all the joy away from me. I don't feel like it's my idea. I feel like it's yours and instead of helping you, now I'm being made to do something. What kind of fun is that?' Of course, over time I've discovered that if I don't ask him, he won't do anything for me. So I'm 'darned if I do and darned if I don't.' "

In talking to Ed we discovered the real reason beneath his apparent unwillingness. In his heart, he harbored the memory of his own father coming home to a sink full of dirty dishes after work each day. In effect, his dad always had to handle the domestic chores, while his mother ran needless errands and talked with her friends. Ed hated seeing his father dominated in this way and determined that the same thing would never happen to him. It was a matter of the old nightmares of his past leaking into present reality.

He rationalizes self-centeredness.

Because of his resistance to any hint of domination, Ed had developed a polished approach to justifying his own inability to consider anybody's needs but his own. His rationalizations were defenses that kept others at a distance and left him firmly in control. If he could keep Sharon reacting to him, rather than acting on her own, then he could continue to live out his self-centered lifestyle. His sermons, his memorized verses, his revelations of past experiences all centered around his needs. Without deliberate thought on his part, he was nonetheless continuing to do what he did best: take care of Ed.

His wife feels dependent and helpless.

Sharon's comments during one of our sessions seemed to sum up the self-doubt and anxieties that her marriage had produced.

"Before I got married I felt independent and confident," she said. "I had a master's degree from a good university and a responsible job for six years after that. But after only a year of marriage, I became helpless and dependent. I was nervous, had no self-assurance at all, didn't know the right thing to say, and it seemed as if I never knew what to do. How could I go so quickly from being a real person to being just a piece of furniture?"

He is distant.

Keeping a comfortable space is a major way that men maintain control. They can leave a problem by walking out the door into their own world, and they can leave it emotionally even when they are home. Solomon—who had more than his share of problems with a thousand wives and whose home must have been a madhouse—writes: "A constant dripping on a day of steady rain and a contentious woman are alike" (Prov. 27:15).

A Woman Can Take Over
(But is she really in control?)

Men who are faced with constant criticism give up. The friction they find when they come home drives them deeper into the sports page and ties them more passively than ever to the TV. Solomon gave up. We detect his hopeless attitude toward the contentious women in his life in Prov. 27:16: "He who would restrain her restrains the wind, and grasps oil with his right hand."

Most men will do anything to avoid confrontation. When confronted at home with never-ending conflict, a man will appear to sound the retreat. Only is it seldom a real retreat. Often, it's an advance in a new direction. He chooses to work late, and so, avoids confrontation. At least at the office he's in control. It's wonderful to be at a job where things can be made to happen. He likes the joy of picking up the phone, punching a number and enjoying instant respect. He knows who he is and that he's in charge.

Some time ago, I watched a couple discuss their difficulties in a counseling session. As she lashed out at her husband, her complaints read like a shopping list: "You come home and just want to lie down. You won't help me with the work. You won't clear the table. You won't bathe the children. You won't take *any* responsibility." Then came the clapper: "If you were a real man, you'd *do* something."

Anyone who would have passed by my window and seen this couple in action would have thought they were viewing the typical hen-pecked husband and his dominating wife.

They would have watched her jab her finger in his direction—and would have arrived at the totally wrong conclusion as to who was actually in control of this home. In spite of her threats, jabs, glares, and all the blows to his manly ego, he remained firmly in control.

For as long as he continued to sit and not respond to her demands, he remained in control. She could rant, rave, rage, beg, plead or promise, but the immovable object was still the center of everyone's attention. He was passively in complete authority.

This withdrawn, passive behavior in men can be essentially a real struggle for control. The passive man can still, very effectively, manage his own life. This type of control, however, removes him from the family. His wife may view his removal as necessary for the orderly function of the home, but what is necessary for the short-term will be devastating to the marriage in the long-term.

As we discussed in chapter 1, God's desire is that each partner in a marriage be a whole person. Both should bring into the relationship an essentially equal and independent personality. This way the two share a ministry with each other in a healthy manner. Let's say that 10 represents a marriage that is contact and collaboration between two complete people. We could illustrate it like this:

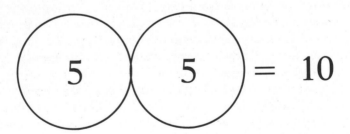

In many cases when a man's position is challenged or thwarted, he will retreat, giving less to the marriage. He may stop bringing his personality, his energy, and his creativity home. A woman's natural tendency then is to assume the space that has been vacated by her husband. She becomes more than she should be in order to make up for his emotional absence and to restore the home to working order.

She initiates conversation because "he won't talk." She takes over all the bill paying because "they'll turn out the lights." She opens the Bible and reads to the children and she prays with them because "my kids won't get anything spiritual from their father." What results is a functioning family unit, but one that's in the process of dying.

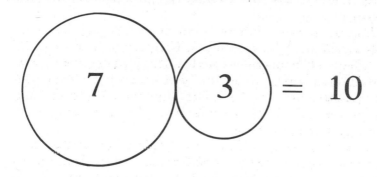

Contact *is* still being made between these people; decisions are being made, bills are being paid, conversations, however inadequate, do occur. Unless the cycle is stopped, though, a woman who spends her life being a seven or an eight when God intended her to be a normal five will become frustrated and fatigued. She becomes trapped. She sees what is happening, but can find no way out.

A man can be content to come home and be a comfortable three. His father may have been a three. Or perhaps the only model he may have had was a dad who showed him how to be a respectable two. Still other men today have fathers who have been totally missing, nonexistent at home. A man in this position usually knows that there is more required to being a good husband and father than what he is giving, but he may be suffering a crisis of confidence. He may feel like a failure, and sees his wife as a constant reminder of his inabilities. He feels accosted by guilt because he won't or doesn't think he can succeed at life. Every good thing she does to fill in the gap is another accusing finger, stabbing in his direction.

These are a few of the major impulses that drive men to

respond to crises in the way they do. Most, of course, are reasons tied to their masculine image.

In the next chapters, we will focus on the differences between men and women and on simple suggestions a wife can use in the process of resigning from the control of her marriage, and so become the equal partner God intended her to be. The process does not offer "instant" success, but it will free a woman to form new, godly habits and new thinking. In fact, it will lead her ever closer to the ultimate goal of her spiritual growth: Christlikeness.

*Men have sight;
women insight*

—Victor Hugo

3

What Makes Men Tick —and Women Tock?

Frank had become so absorbed in his newspaper he hardly noticed his wife, Samantha, passing him with her second load of grocery bags—not until she blasted him. "Don't you see I've got two arms full of groceries? I've had a hard day at work and had to pick up the kids, too. You just come home and lie there with your newspaper. Get with it, *mister.*"

Frank lowered the sports page long enough to see the eyes of his two children soaking it all in. Their mother had yelled at them in the supermarket and in the car—and now she was yelling at their dad. He felt diminished in their eyes—like nothing more than a big kid.

As he listened to her tirade, which soon turned into an icy silence, during which she resisted his caresses and attempts to make up, Frank wondered why he had come home at all. If he had just worked late, as usual, he could have skipped this whole miserable scene. What was the big deal about carrying in a few bags of groceries?

Samantha, on the other hand, fumed silently all evening— with the same question: What was so hard about helping her carry in a few bags of groceries? Why did Frank always leave it up to her—along with most of the other household chores?

As I counseled with Frank and Samantha, one fact became clear at once: neither one seemed to understand what his or her partner really needed in life. Therefore, they had made a lifelong pattern of assuming certain things about each other. Frank expected that "Sam," as he called her, would keep up with the housework, even while holding down another job. After all, she was a woman. He would never have admitted to that kind of thinking with the women executives in his office, but he never stopped to think that his wife was a woman who worked in an office just like the women he encountered at his own office.

Somehow, Frank never considered all these factors: When Samantha got home from her job, she was just as tired as he was. She had a long commute, during which she planned the evening's meal. She stopped at the store, then headed home to the hot stove that awaited the end of a long day.

In fact, each of them viewed their time at home from a completely different perspective. Frank saw it as a time when he could have "space to breathe"; she saw it as a time when they could build their relationship through working together and conversation. Neither one had guessed that their ability to accept and love each other should be based partly on their insights into the differences between men and women.

With so little understanding of each other's motivations, it was no wonder they were frustrated and confused. A union that began in their church college group when they were young and full of hopes had become a marriage of disappointment. Frank saw a wife who did not appreciate him, did not respond to him sexually, and who did not try to understand his needs. He felt constantly nagged. Samantha saw an insensitive man who thought only of himself and who was growing colder and more distant by the day. "I understand him all right," she complained. "That's my problem—what I understand, I don't like!"

This portrait—a husband and wife alienated by gender differences—is not the picture God had in mind at creation. The contradictions that allured us to our mates change too soon from fascination to frustration. We move from delighting in our spouses to demanding that they think, talk, and act as we do. We forget to focus on their obvious strengths and, instead, highlight the irritation of their differences.

The factors that push marriage into an emotional drift are largely issues of maleness and femaleness. We misunderstand each other and can, over a period of time, lazily assume the wrong things about how to relate to each other. Refocusing our attention from the negative to the positive is the first basic step in stopping the hurts and misunderstandings that eat away at a marriage.

Along with a renewed attitude, husbands and wives can make other positive steps toward the rebuilding of their relationship into a strong, healthy marriage. These steps must be based on a clear understanding, not only of sexual differences, but of how the different sexes prefer to be treated when it comes to building self-esteem, the different meanings we assign to the same words, and the different goals each is trying to achieve.

Differences in How We Build Self-esteem

The concept of self-esteem is often misunderstood by Christians. It has been painted with the brush of self-*love* and, repeatedly, we as believers have been told to look upon it as another worldly value thrust upon an unsuspecting Christian community. But self-love (or self-exaltation) is different from having self-esteem—which simply means to have a *proper, balanced* view of ourselves. The fact that we are made in God's image is a gift, something we can neither earn nor renounce.

And while God wants us to know that we are "good" creations and highly valued, there are several tendencies in the way men and women come to this balanced, healthy view of themselves.

Dr. James Dobson in his compelling book *Hide, or Seek?*, which traces the development of self-esteem in children, focuses on the aspects of beauty and intelligence. Both of these are gifts of God and not our own achievements. Yet, so much of how we see ourselves is caught up in the whirlpool of competition over these gifts. These two attributes, he points out, are unequally prized by men and women:

> For men, physical attractiveness gradually sub-

merges as a value during late adolescence and early adulthood, yielding first place to intelligence. For women, however, beauty retains its number-one position throughout life, even into middle age and beyond. *The reason the average woman would rather have beauty than brains is that she knows the average man can see better than he can think.* Her value system is based on his and will probably continue that way.[1]

So, even at the basic level, men and woman are both threatened and rewarded by pursuing different goals.

Where We Build Our Self-esteem

I was startled one day by Monica as she blurted out, "I've got a problem. My husband is in bed with his boss." The shocked expression on my face must have assured her she had my full attention. "Oh, I don't mean for real," she went on. "But it seems that way. He's more concerned with pleasing that man than with pleasing me. Richard just can't turn down an assignment. He even volunteers to do a job when he knows it's going to conflict with our home life. What should I do?"

Richard, I later learned, had a number of reasons why he was giving extra attention to work. He saw a promotion possibility. There was a boom in his business that was causing everyone to work overtime, and he saw all the pressures as only temporary bends in the flow of the healthy routine. Monica, on the other hand, was aiming her efforts at the home and family. Neither of them could see that their lives were being built in two different places—places that each thought the other had little understanding or sympathy for.

Now, it's true that many men love to work around their home. Many love to cook. My own mother seldom felt she could compete with Dad in the kitchen. But few men would choose gardening or cooking over a bleacher seat at their child's Little League game. And most men would prefer lunch with their wife instead of lunch with the boss. But a man seldom receives a promotion for perfect attendance at Little

---

[1]James Dobson, *Hide, or Seek?* (Old Tappan, N.J.: Fleming H. Revell, 1974), 43.

League or a savory spaghetti dinner. Therefore the average man won't check out early from work so he can go grocery shopping with his wife. His work, the place where his self-esteem is built, is largely found outside of his home.

Given only the options of success or failure, a man who is successful at work—and yet whose marriage is a failure and whose children are ill-behaved—will consider himself a success. Conversely, a woman in similar circumstances will usually see herself as a failure. This is because they have different worlds and build their self-esteem in separate locations. A man is caught up with what he *does* in life. His wife is far more concerned with the *relationships* that make living worthwhile.

Listening carefully to a gathering of men and women who have just met will demonstrate what I mean. Even a woman who works will tend to discuss her family. Work, to her, is the means, not the end.

A man, on the other hand, seldom introduces himself, saying, "Hi. I'm the father of two daughters." He views himself in terms of what he does or what he owns, his hobbies, titles, clubs, church and his car. In short, *a man's significance is found in what he has authority over.* His work is the only way he knows of keeping all those items under his control.

Work also lets him know how he connects with his world. Work allows him to feel he is connected to something greater than his own life. To be needed and vital to a job is a sensation that gives a man a rush of adrenaline. He may hide those feelings with moans about what he cannot do with his family because he is working, but he would never exchange those postponed activities for unemployment.

But that "something greater" at work takes its toll on a man. It is important, therefore, for a woman to see that her husband's world of conflict at the office dumps a needy man on her doorstep each night. He is someone who needs to be ministered to. His inadequacy cannot be entirely satisfied with Little League or a little chat.

As Monica and Richard talked, it became apparent that she believed Richard thought his job was more important than their life together, and that he believed Monica had lost respect for him. "She doesn't know or doesn't care what I do all day," he answered. "My boss is more concerned about her than she is about him, and *we're* the Christians!"

When Richard came home he saw himself entering Monica's world. It was his home too, but he felt the activities there were her major concern and in her control. This couple faced the task of learning to see life from each other's contradictory point of view.

For the woman who wants to begin entering her husband's world, a good starting point is to ask, "Where can I have a ministry *in that world?*" Richard was stunned when Monica asked, "What can I pray about today, for your work?" From that point, it moved to asking if prayers for work were being answered, then to an occasional short phone call at lunch hour, then to praying together in the mornings before he raced to the freeway. It was only natural that Richard soon began to connect himself to Monica's daily undertakings as well.

Marriage is intended to be a spiritual operation where each partner sees an opportunity to meet needs in their own home, *and in the world,* through the other. When a husband, who is designed to take the initiative, elects instead to pursue his own personal goals, hitting the ceiling is by far the most counterproductive thing a wife can do.

Differences in Language

Not long ago I asked a group of thirty Christian couples to describe the differences between men and women. Most of the answers centered on communication:

- He does not pay attention to the details of daily life routines—things take care of themselves, find themselves, clean themselves, etc.
- Women tend to include emotional influences in all decisions whether or not the topic has great emotional impact. Men talk about the action they would take, and believe that the topic was fully discussed.
- Men take more time to make decisions because some men are not as intelligent as women. (Women just hide theirs.)
- Women don't come right to the point!
- Women seem so sensitive—they react before knowing

the real background or meaning of some of the words.
- He doesn't have very much emotion.
- Men do not seem to be aware of problems until they are personally affected, *even if their mate has been trying to make them aware of it.*

A telling response from one man points out the major problem: *"I never gave it much thought."*

First Peter 3 contains a marvelous set of instructions for husbands and wives on how to relate to each other. It is not accidental that the Apostle Peter summarizes his instructions on how to be happily married with these words:

> Whoever wants to enjoy life and see delightful days must keep his tongue from evil and his lips from speaking deceit. (1 Pet. 3:10, Williams NT)

The notebooks of marriage counselors are filled with words that should never have been spoken.

The genuine measure of our communication in marriage is not found in what we say but in what we hear. On that score, all couples fall somewhere between captivated and bewildered.

Let's consider some of the main differences in the way women use words.

Women are more supportive in conversation.

When listening to conversation between spouses, several startling differences appear. A woman gives both verbal and nonverbal support as the man talks about himself. A husband appears to listen less well and seldom asks his wife to discuss experiences.

A man will often interrupt a conversation that involves women.

In a group of men *or* women, the conversation is matched and well paced and interruptions are kept to a minimum, but a mixed group is frequently interrupted by a man.

A woman often spices her statements with a leading question, "Have you ever wondered why . . . etc."

Many statements are given in a rising tone of voice that suggests a question or leaves room for further rejoinder. In natural conversation, she has also mastered the use of queries that draw people out. Questioning is a distinctive ingredient of female speech.

The clash that most often rises from this distinctive female speech habit occurs when a husband comes home after an especially difficult day. His schedule may have contained a glut of demands for instant responses to people and situations. He comes home ready for a quiet evening. He may want to hear statements or news from his wife, but no questions or demands. His wife may need to make some demands on him, but when combined with her normal style of supportive conversation, it all becomes too much for him to handle.

Women hear emotionally; men tend to hear only the facts.

When thinking of how men listen, the picture is similar to *Dragnet*, the police program of long ago. Sgt. Friday would stand with his silent partner at a door, asking a woman questions. Each detective was armed with a notebook and a cool, emotionless stare.

Friday would listen to the lady sensationally recounting the crime and drawing into her story assumptions, impressions, and guesses about why the person did what she saw him do. Friday would then snap, "Just the facts, ma'am, just the facts!"

Because the aspect of relationship is often an afterthought to men, they have difficulty mixing fact with feeling, or seeing the emotional consequences of what they do. A man may know his second job will give him X amount of dollars; he can also project that, along with his wife's income, they will earn enough money to make a down payment on their dream home in only two years. But he overlooks the tension his wife feels about their own relationship. She sees the impending disaster due to the lack of time he is spending with their teenaged son. As she thinks about their plans, she is busy balancing a new home with the potentially crippled family moving into it.

Romantic and Sexual Satisfaction

Sex itself and the approach to sexuality present big differences between men and women.

A woman would rarely separate romance and sex. For her, sex is a reflection of her life as a whole. Nagging problems with bills, a lack of her husband's romantic interest, and the totality of the day's events make up the disposition of her sexual desire.

"Pat never understood this," said Jill, who was thirty-eight, and had been married for twelve years. "He'd come home, go right to the mail and then plop down in front of the TV for the duration of the evening. When the news was over at 11:30, he'd feel frisky, and by then I was out of gas. Even if I felt like it, I'd have liked a little polite conversation first. Pat would say, 'We can talk later.' But that didn't make sex very enjoyable. I felt cheap!"

For women, sex is not an event, but a whole-life orientation.

As with most men, Pat's idea of sex was goal-oriented. To him, sex was an event. "Why can't a woman just enjoy sex for the sake of the moment," he complained. "Can't she just forget the rest of the day even for a little bit?"

To Jill, good sex reflected their life together as a whole. If she was tired, or had enjoyed no decent conversation with Pat in days, her sexual desire was low. If Pat communicated by his busyness or his attitude, "I want sex with you, but I just don't want to talk to you or spend time with you," Jill saw herself as his convenience, not his wife. The idea infuriated rather than stimulated her.

In the sexual encounter, men and women have different objectives.

For a man, the objective of sex often seems limited to orgasm. There are, however, a number of other "hidden agendas."

The first is *confirmation of his masculinity.* The most difficult hurdle for a man to leap is the correlation of his masculinity with his ability to perform sexually. George Gilder makes this statement in his thought-provoking book *Men and Marriage*:

> In modern society, sexual relations with women are becoming the chief way men assert their sexual iden-

tity. But in most of the world's societies, sexual relations follow achievement of manhood, or accompany it.[2]

Second, sex accomplishes *the affirmation of his ego*. When a man's wife responds to his advances, his ego is stroked. For one who is near or past mid-life, that is crucial. He desperately needs reassurance that life is not in the past tense, but here and now. His sex life gives instant evidence of that fact.

This agenda is similar for women. A woman also wants her ego built and her femininity affirmed. Her method, however, makes closeness and love the objective. Sexual orgasm is only one of many building blocks in the achievement of that goal. The continuous rhythm of her life and relationships are, for her, a greater measure of love and closeness.

The subject of sex was rarely discussed by Pat and Jill, though. And when it was, it was never discussed rationally. When Pat's demands were spurned, he got angry or he sulked. Jill would then find herself responding out of pity. Both ended their lovemaking feeling cheated of what they wanted most in their relationship: care and respect.

When it comes to sexuality, communication can be most tricky. A woman feels intimidated about sharing what she needs in the sexual relationship, because any suggestion sounds like a criticism. After all, to a man, sex is not just a biological and emotional need; it is an ego need. Criticism can be devastating, so timing is crucial. The most helpful time to discuss these issues is when a wife can bring up the subject. That is the way Pat and Jill learned to resolve their problem.

"Sweetheart, I really want to have a good sexual life with you," Jill would begin. "I know you're not a mind reader, so I'd like you to help me to be more free to enjoy it." Asking him to help her (when the discussion did not center on what he was doing wrong at the time) was the best start she could hope for. It allowed them as a couple to begin to build their understanding of each other in a nonthreatening way. Just this simple change of phrasing, with attention to timing, helped them on the road to a more fulfilling love life.

---

[2]George Gilder, *Men and Marriage* (Gretna, La.: Pelican Publishing, 1986), 27.

Competition: The Endless Male Tournament

No discussion of maleness can overlook the competitive nature of men, and where this nature comes from.

Men cut their teeth on competition. Part of this nature is God-given, a parcel in the emotional equipment that is necessary for a man to protect his family in a hostile world. When studying this subject, we should be careful to recognize that differences between men and women are elements of creation that exist for a *purpose*.

How women and men compete is often a by-product of training.

Little girls are often coached on how to lose to boys. The aggressive spirit in young boys that draws smiles and praise is often frowned upon when displayed by their sisters. As young women grow up, they are told, "Men prefer women who don't kill their own snakes." In many respects women become "closet competitors." The urge to come out on top is still there, but most women feel the need to apologize for it.

My wife, for instance, was encouraged to lose the majority of chess games to gentlemen callers. As she thought it over, she realized, "When those guys left to go home, I'd still have to live with myself. So, no thanks!" (I still avoid playing chess with her!)

Competition—the bad side of it—displays an element of our fallen nature.

A distinct element of pride makes this competitive aspect of mankind's fallen nature distinctly masculine. It presents itself as a great temptation at every level, even among pastors. At conferences they can and do begin matching ministries. When they confide in one another, comparison and competition are among their greatest temptations.

The Apostle Paul deftly sidestepped being drawn into this trap. In 2 Cor. 10:12, he aims at the heartbeat of pride in every man:

> For we are not bold to class or compare ourselves with some of those who commend themselves; but when they *measure themselves by themselves, and com-*

*pare themselves with themselves, they are without under-
standing.* (Italics added)

Competition is a factor of our culture.
A cultural aspect of male competition rears its head in our
individualistic Western society. We live in a civilization
founded and expanded by "rugged individualists." In years
past, every man's boyhood hero was a self-made man who
carved out adventure by the sheer force of his will. We have
also been drilled to "stand out from the herd." But along with
the benefits of excellence, there is an emotional price to pay.

Not all cultures exhibit this same fascination with being
"on top." Several years ago, I spoke to a conference of Asian
single adults in Hawaii. They represented several age groups:
some were in careers, some were college students, a few were
in high school, and several were of junior-high age. As I observed these young people, I could not distinguish any separation of age groups by the way they treated one another.

They were also divided into competitive teams; they scored
points for everything from keeping their cabins clean to the
performance of team skits. I was stunned as they applauded
enthusiastically for one another during the events and the final judging. By watching the audience, I could not tell who
belonged to which team. It was unlike any group in my experience on the mainland. As it was explained to me, "In our
culture, family is important. If one does well, we all succeed."

In the West, however, many men feel a surge of competition
when they enter the working world, and some even act out
their conquests on social and spiritual levels. This leaves them
lonely and often exhausted beyond what might reasonably be
expected by their effort. It also greatly inhibits their willing-
ness to have their feelings, insecurities, and failures made
known—even to their wives.

This symptom is a great frustration to women. "Why can't
he *tell* me how he feels? I didn't know he was frustrated at
work. Is it because he doesn't trust me, or is it because I'm
just not that important in his life?" The answer to these questions lies with his lack of communication skills and lack of
practice at sharing feelings.

Dependency: The Masculine Soft Spot

A man may outwardly seem the model of bravado and security. Even his fantasies may be filled with illusions of the carefree single life and "playing the field." But for a man, carefree singleness is only that—an illusion, a mirage in the midst of the desert. God knew what He was doing when Adam was by himself in the garden and God said, "It is *not good* for man to be alone."

My own experience as a widower, in the early seventies, showed how "shell-shocked" a single man could become. Shortly after my first wife's death, I left my career in the Air Force to return to college. In my mid-twenties, exposed to a new social life, I never dated. I would absorb myself instead with study. I did not go for walks—I went for wanders, aimlessly prowling, seeing sights that I wished I could share with my wife. Each day seemed pointless.

My friends who knew my first wife had the mistaken impression that because she was frequently hospitalized, she was dependent on me. In truth, I was emotionally dependent on her. As a man, I wasn't emotionally equipped to handle separation. This competitive world that always demands a man prove himself had left me lonely and dependent.

It is this trait of emotional dependency that can propel a husband into passivity. The need to be "mothered" and the hankering of his ego to be first place in someone else's life shapes an emotional whirlpool of dependency. For a woman to keep in balance the role of help-meet without becoming a "second mother" is tricky. To avoid the destructiveness of over-mothering, a woman should ask herself these questions:

- Am I solving problems that are his?
- Am I creating a habit for him of always asking me for the solution?
- Am I trying to make him dependent for my ego needs?
- Do I view him as someone I respect and can rely on?
- Do I view my husband as someone who is growing old or someone who is growing up?

The next two chapters will show why these question are important to a marriage, and what to do if you find you are not happy with their answers.

Seven Watchmen sitting in a tower,
Watching what had come upon mankind,
Showed the man the glory and the power,
And bade him shape the kingdom of his mind.

—Kipling

4

The Building Blocks of Passive Resistance

Tom and Cindy married before they became friends.

They met in a church singles group, attracted to each other from across the room. Even without speaking, Cindy said she knew. "*This* was the guy. I'd dated many men and knew what I was looking for."

Maybe it was this overconfidence at finding Mr. Right, especially in a church, that caused Cindy to neglect getting to know Tom. Now, though they were not sorry they had gotten married, they were in pain. They were each in the midst of an emotional crisis that had been building since they were young. Their marriage was at a critical juncture, as if they'd been carefully developing this crisis according to some unwritten plan.

Tom said to me, "I knew I needed a wife. I'd graduated, was working on my master's degree and had a good job at a growing company. I'd been in love before, but now the time was right. Cindy was attractive, someone I knew I could love. I guess the problem is just me. The harder I work and the more I try to do, the more unhappy she gets."

As we talked, the pattern of daily life for Tom and Cindy emerged. Tom was working at a chemical engineering job and pursuing a master's degree two nights a week. He and Cindy attended a Bible study and were active at their church. Cindy worked, but then when she came home she felt as if she had another full-time job, caring for the house and for Tom. They seldom talked. Tom studied and watched TV. The more Cindy begged for his attention, the more Tom studied and stayed late at work. Tom's standard response to her complaints was, "Why can't she just accept me as I am? I don't know why I can't be everything she wants. All I know how to be is *me.*"

Tom's rationale, which I restated to him, went like this: "I am what I am. I didn't make myself this way. I can't become everything she wants me to be. So if I can't change, then she must." This is a very common defense among couples: If one spouse can point the finger of accountability at the other, then the guilt they feel becomes easier to deal with.

It is often said, "Practice makes perfect." In truth, practice doesn't make *perfect*: it makes *permanent*! Wrong habit patterns are rooted in a lifetime of wrong thinking. A man does not change his reactions when he changes his mailing address and moves in from his parents' home. Old thinking patterns and their resultant habits continue long after the wedding. Often a wife's response to them—nagging, anger, manipulation and guilt projection—only compounds the problem and deepens the husband's unspoken conclusion: "Home is *not* where I want to be."

How good it is to know that God is committed to changing our thought processes. Second Cor. 10:4–5 discusses the power of change that is at work in the life of every believer, and reveals how that power springs from our thinking:

> For the weapons of our warfare are not of the flesh, but divinely powerful for the destruction of fortresses. We are destroying speculations and every lofty thing raised up against the knowledge of God, and *we are taking every thought captive to the obedience of Christ.* (Italics added.)

For Tom and Cindy the building blocks of wrong thinking began early in childhood.

Conflict at Home

In Tom's childhood and Cindy's, too, home was always a battlefield. Their earliest memories were like reports from a war zone. There were pleasant times at home; but over all, tension reigned.

Cindy's father had grown up on a farm with eight brothers, a hard-working father and an overbearing mother. As a husband, he loved his family, but he was determined never to allow himself to lose control of his own home. Cindy never saw her father apologize and never heard him admit wrong. "I'm sorry" was not in his vocabulary. When he was obviously wrong, Cindy, her mother and two sisters would look knowingly at each other without uttering a word. Later, Cindy's dad would try to balance the scales of justice with the wife or daughter he had offended. He would buy her something or do something nice for her. No word was spoken about the original offense, but everyone knew the reason for the gift.

Most important to note, at no time did her father give up control of the situation to a female. Whenever Dad spoke, that was the final decree—no appeal, no reasoning, only a verdict. Cindy saw her mother live a pleasant life—but never as an equal partner in the marriage.

When Cindy met Tom and listened to his goals in life, she was attracted, at least in part, by his strong motivation and his ability to determine right from wrong. Not conscious of the similarities between Tom and her father, something "felt right" about Tom. His patterns and his thinking made her feel "at home."

Quite the opposite of Cindy, Tom's mother had been the decision-maker in his childhood home. She was better educated than his awkward, self-effacing father. His father had no high school diploma, few social graces and always seemed awkward in social situations. As Tom grew up, watching his dominated and seemingly helpless father, he told himself, "I never want to be like that. I don't want to be at other people's mercy—especially the mercy of my wife." Yet for Tom, living with a woman who wanted control made him feel "at home."

The problems were not obvious to Cindy immediately. She had learned to live with a distant man who would not communicate. Her father would not be vulnerable. He felt the need to be in control at all times. Therefore, as irritated as she grew with Tom and his passive and distant behavior, her responses to him were all too familiar. Though she hated the feeling it gave her, she became more aggressive and complaining.

It's not uncommon—in fact it's quite logical—that men and women tend to marry someone who makes them feel "at home." Studies have shown that women who come from dysfunctional families often marry men like their fathers. Some studies have shown that as many as 60 percent of the women who marry alcoholics have come from a home with an alcoholic father. Something attracts them to these men, beckoning them to finish in their own husbands what their mothers were unable to accomplish with their fathers. Many women, like Cindy, will marry someone like Dad. On the other hand, it is just as common for a man to be attracted to a woman who runs the house, because that is all he has ever known.

Mel Roman and Patricia Raley address this phenomenon in their appropriately titled book *The Indelible Family*:

> The family identity does not have to be positive to be cohesive. Many families find that special feeling from their problems. Families that have no special identity are not cohesive and will probably break up. But most families form a bond by reaching for whatever gives them an identity of their own.[1]

A Hostile World View

Unfortunately, the bond that gives many families cohesiveness—if it can be called that—is a very negative view of life. And the hostility with which many homes have been endowed comes from hostile perceptions—perceptions started in the living room or around the dining table.

In his book *More Communication Keys for Your Marriage*, Norman Wright observes:

> For many of us, unresolved relationships and issues

---

[1]Mel Roman and Patricia Raley, *The Indelible Family* (New York: Rawson Wade Pub., 1980), 16.

of the past are still guiding our lives and hampering communication. Some of us even suffer because of a half-resolved and half-buried past. Because we react and respond to others on the basis of unresolved past relationships, we actually perpetuate those difficulties. Some of us carry wounds from the past; some carry scars. Some of us have buried our painful memories hoping those memories never resurrect.[2]

Those buried wounds are easily reopened by an unsuspecting spouse who had no hand in creating the pain. For a man who is filled with painful self-doubt brought on by his hostile past, the enemy is not just the person who created the scar, but the person who reminds him it is there. The same, of course, can by true of women.

Inadequate or Missing Role Models for Men

Historically, when we were an agricultural nation, what a father *did* was apparent to everyone in the household. There was never any doubt as to what it took to be a man—it took hard work, dedication and an ability to adjust to changing weather and circumstances. Today, when Dad leaves the house for work, he sequesters himself in a walled building where little boys and girls are deprived of the opportunity to see masculinity in action. Their only opportunity to view it is when he arrives home ten hours later, exhausted and hungry, too tired to communicate and wanting only to slump in front of the TV.

A popular phrase that repeats itself in Christian circles— too often in an attempt to justify the amount of time we are *not* spending with our children—is the term "quality time." It is used to justify a heavy travel schedule and long hours at the office; the promise of some future "quality time" will supposedly make it all better. The term is used to describe a planned event for the family that is blueprinted to be "meaningful." In a child's mind, all time is quality time; and if he has to miss out on the normal times with his father in order to be ap-

---

[2]Norman Wright, *More Communication Keys for Your Marriage* (Ventura, Calif.: Regal Books), 48–49.

peased with special events, he will be unsatisfied.

Taking a child on errands, showing him the office on a Saturday, talking and praying around the breakfast table—these are just as meaningful and can be far more frequent than "quality time."

In the case of Tom and Cindy, Tom had very, very little time with his father who was a machine-shop worker. He was highly respected by the men who worked with him because of the quality of his work. Unfortunately, Tom had been to his father's shop only once and never had an opportunity to talk with his father's fellow workers to hear them praise his dad. This entire area of his father's life was closed off to Tom. The only father he saw was the socially awkward man who came home to be dominated by Tom's mother. It was an unrealistic picture of the man, but it was the picture of manhood that lingered in Tom's mind. By neglect, sons are taught that to be a man today means to be away from home, in a world of uncertainty, and then to come home too tired to talk.

Boys like Tom are being raised by women with too much day-to-day power over their lives. Without a father who takes a strong hand to help them adjust to life with mother, the young boy naturally overcompensates and, in time, forms formidable defenses *against* women in general. These defenses will not be abandoned when he marries.

Loneliness

Tom's father, in his quest for job security, moved the family on numerous occasions. Tom, his brother and sisters attended eight different schools. He became accustomed to being a stranger and an outsider. What's more, in observing his father's financial dilemma, he told himself that the secret to true happiness lay in job security and affluence, never grasping the need for friendship and commitment. The skills of self-disclosure and trust in people were never formed as he developed each new set of temporary friends. It was no mystery why sharing his feelings with Cindy was more difficult than it should have been and why, when he did, it was superficial.

The Missing Male-Friendship Factor

In America, our mobile lifestyle makes it difficult at best to make friends. Certainly this is the case for men. But men become sold on the notion that a satisfying job and a promotion will give them money; therefore, they won't need friends.

Women seem fascinated by a man's special world. To a housewife especially, her husband's job seems like a glamorous encounter with the bustling business world. But a woman who works outside of the home knows this is not entirely the case. At times, these women also desire to belong to the clubs and social circles of their male counterparts. It appears, on the surface, that men are friendly and their conversations and interaction stimulating. Perhaps this impression comes, in part, from beer commercials on television—whenever a beer is opened, friendship and good times among men seem to flow. The reality, however, is that this kind of camaraderie is far from the norm.

Friendship skills are a problem with men. In a group of sixty Christian couples, I asked the men the following questions: Who is your best friend? How long has it been since you last saw him? Over 90 percent of the responses cited a relationship of the past—a college chum, a friend in the military, or "Sam, my best buddy in the seventh grade." These "historical friendships" form the bulk of what men choose to call close relationships.

Women find it far easier to disclose themselves to other women. They talk to one another about tensions in their marriage, problems and questions related to child-rearing and the lack of fulfillment at work. But to men, each of these issues would represent a failure that few men are willing to admit. A man's sense of competition and the need to appear successful makes disclosure a labor of trust. Most do not have a relationship with any other man that allows them to confide in any way.

Should a Man's Best Friend Be His . . . *Wife*?

Many Christians assume that a man's best friend *should* be his wife. While that is the objective and the foundation for every good marriage, the importance of male friendships cannot be minimized. A wife may view her husband's recreation and conversation with another man as stealing his time with her. But in fact, it enriches and protects their relationship. It will allow him to validate his feelings in comparison to those of other men. Ultimately, having a male confidant can even protect him from an affair.

A man's feelings are his most vulnerable area, and when he shares them he usually chooses to do so with someone who can give him the tenderness and sympathy he desires. It is natural and healthy that the person who extends that type of support be his wife. But if the pain he is feeling is related to something *she* is doing to him or not doing for him, then the easiest thing for him to do is to confide his problems to another woman. *Without a doubt, this is a dangerous course of action.* To have a male friend with whom he can talk about his needs in confidence is to have a healthy outlet for growth and protection.

A male friend will also help him to grow in the ability to share his emotions. A husband may share his feelings with his wife; but if he is unsure of himself or what he is thinking or feeling, he will need a male sounding board for his emotions. While he may appreciate and need his wife's listening ear and offer of sympathy, at the same time he thinks, "She's a woman—how could she know what I'm supposed to feel?" After baring his soul to his wife, the husband will still be faced with the questions, "Am I okay? Did I do the right thing?" In *The Secrets Men Keep*, Dr. Ken Druck says:

> Once we open our world to another man, we learn that we are not alone in our fears, insecurities, uncertainties and desires. Nothing is *wrong* with us, as we might have secretly suspected. Through a friendship with another man, we affirm much of what is good and strong in us as men. Frank and honest exchanges of experiences allow us to gain a fresh and clear perspective on ourselves.[3]

The only place where a man can reasonably afford to be

[3]Dr. Ken Druck, *The Secrets Men Keep* (Garden City, N.Y.: Doubleday & Co., 1985), 104.

honest with other people is in the Christian community. In spite of all the horror stories heard about people who did just that and lived to regret it, there simply is no other place where confession and forgiveness are considered virtues. The Christian community is also one of the few places were a man can hope to find help from his peers. In the general population, men tend to express only their successes so they can be assured of approval. But the Christian community—while it sometimes falls short of what it should be—more often helps men and women to bear up during hard times. In Prov. 17:17 Solomon declares: "A friend loves at all times, and a brother is born for adversity."

The more a man has his feelings confirmed by another man, the greater will be his capacity to risk himself and his feelings with his wife. Far from losing out with the time her husband spends with other men, his wife will be the chief beneficiary.

Wrong Values

Another characteristic of the passive husband is that he frequently bases his thinking on wrong values. He may not necessarily be passive about life; he just seems preoccupied with "other things" and is passive about life *at home*. He is busily building an emotional nest of his own with the twigs and branches of wrong values. A lifetime of seeing relationships at home as unsatisfying, added to the lack of a male success story at home and a sense of loneliness, have left him with only one set of achievements by which to measure himself: He buys into the notion that to be an outward success and an inward failure is still, at "the bottom line," to be a success.

Tom's parents had told him many times: "To get ahead in this world, you've got to get a good education." Tom's father blamed his own unhappiness on the lack of an education and a good job. Tom became convinced that the pursuit of a good education was a man's most important goal. To Tom, success in college took on another, subliminal meaning: If he succeeded, it would mean he was a "better" man than his father.

The result of such thinking showed in his schedule and in the way he drove himself to operate at peak performance all the time.

Not content with a normal pace of study while in college, Tom sped up the process and carried double the number of classes his adviser suggested. Each Tuesday and Wednesday, he left home at dawn with a sack lunch and a sack dinner, so Cindy did not see him at all from late Monday to late Wednesday evening. Their communication was past the point of merely suffering. Cindy came to see herself as little more than an indentured servant who typed, not a real person who had needs of her own. To Tom, that diploma was a symbol of success. He was radar-locked in the process of proving his manhood and his value in the only way he had been taught.

People with wrong values are obsessed with stockpiling symbols: a luxury car, a job title, exotic vacations. Their life's goal is to possess the appropriate *chic* icons by which to measure their worth. These *things* represent to them an objective measurement of status and power. For a man who has grown up feeling powerless, the temptation to latch hold of these things becomes irresistible.

When money, possessions and status are held up as the most accurate measure of success, the competitive man will try his best to reach for those laurels. Our entire advertising industry is built upon the notion of instilling *dis*satisfaction. Promoters and hucksters want you and me to believe that we should not be content with what we have presently. The ads they devise are designed to convince us that to belong to the intellectual, financial, or beautiful elite, we must drive *their* car or wear *their* jacket.

The childishness of wrong values has long roots and bitter fruit. Only acceptance by God based on the saving work of His Son can free us to give ourselves to other people and to find belonging in His fellowship and theirs.

Now, set these wrong values next to the related building blocks of passiveness, and the shaky foundation is set. For any man who has gathered these unstable habits of thinking, there arises a need to try to maintain absolute control over a life that refuses to be managed well.

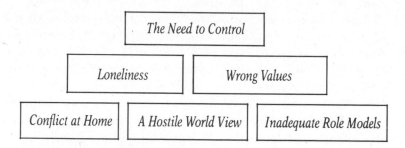

The Need to Control		
Loneliness		Wrong Values
Conflict at Home	A Hostile World View	Inadequate Role Models

The Need for Control

For many a man, being in charge—specifically, being in control of the woman in his life—is a consuming passion. To Tom, control over Cindy was more than a passion: it was, in his view, necessary for emotional survival. His fear of the power that women had over him was something of which he was desperate to rid himself.

A vast array of problems face a man who feels a compulsive need for control. Much has been covered in Chapter 2, devoted entirely to this issue. Yet, the link between this need and the make up of the passive man is important to establish.

One who is fearful of women and feels comfortable only with those he can control is a prime candidate to become a first-class casanova. Every woman he conquers ceases to be a threat to his masculinity, "proving" his manhood, about which he has much doubt.

Tom also faced another problem, though: Because of Cindy's home life as a child, she had promised she would never disappear under a man's domination. When she looked at Tom, she saw only a man pursuing his own dream—a dream she had never factored in when she stood with him at the altar. She married *Tom*; she didn't marry his wild notion of being a man of many degrees in pursuit of the perfect job.

Conversely, when Tom looked at Cindy and listened to her demands for more attention, he saw his mother. Cindy was just another woman who wanted to dominate him.

These conflicting views touched off a chain reaction. Cindy subconsciously saw in Tom her father's obstinate need to dominate the agenda of the house. She reacted wildly to the thought of a husband who would not communicate with her or treat her as a equal partner in the marriage. Therefore, the reservoir of negative feelings about her father that had been carefully stored through the years poured out on someone who only partially deserved it: Tom.

A couple with a history made up of these factors may continue to survive. They cope and wait for better times—better times that never come. They try retreats, Bible studies, deeper-life disciplines and many other ways to get around having to change. They may struggle to keep up appearances. Those Band-Aid solutions may even work—temporarily. But all too predictably, a crisis will bring down the house of cards and, mercifully, force them to deal with the problem.

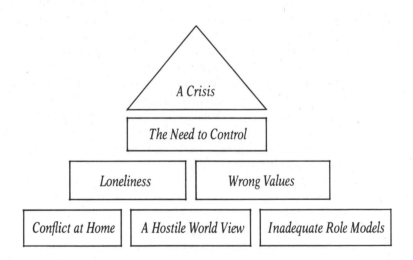

A Crisis of Confidence

It was a crisis that brought Tom and Cindy to me.

Tom's company was overjoyed when he completed his degree. His office threw a party. Cindy was present, and the people at the division where he worked were pleased that Tom had gone out of his way to become better prepared for the job. What neither Tom nor his boss knew on that day was that circumstances were developing that would soon cripple their entire industry. The wonderful celebration was to become a bloodbath of layoffs only six months later.

When the dismissals were announced, Tom sat down with his boss to determine how long he might have to wait to be rehired. It was then the full extent of the crisis hit.

Tom was surprised to learn that not only would he lose his job, but during the years of his stressful studies there had been a series of complaints about him by his fellow workers. The people working around him felt that he was not only competitive but constantly trying to show them up. They had also noted a great deal of anger and hostility and Tom's inability to handle the slightest problem without feeling threatened. When they worked with him, they sensed that it was too important for him to be in charge and to get the credit.

The list of grievances staggered Tom, but as we talked the pattern became obvious. What had happened to Tom at work had been devastating for his employment, but as the thing turned out it would prove lifesaving for his marriage. He and Cindy finally got down to the core of their inability to communicate. From there, they were able to begin working on their marriage in honesty and openness.

As long as we can safely lie to ourselves and believe that our wrong values will work, we seem to squeak by. But in the long run, God in His mercy will not allow us to escape into wrong pursuits. There is the law of the harvest that Senator Sam Erwin quoted as he closed the Watergate hearing and brought down the gavel on the presidency of Richard Nixon:

> Do not be deceived, God is not mocked; for whatever
> a man sows, this he will also reap. (Gal. 6:7)

That same principle applies to everyone, from the Chief

Executive to the lowest office boy. When the crisis does occur, it exposes an entire network of wrong thinking. In the end, a crisis can serve to help a man take down the walls and allow himself to reach out for long-needed help. Then, many couples find that life together can begin again.

For man is born for trouble, as sparks fly upward.

—Job 5:7

5

The Withdrawn Man

It is in the basic nature of a man to assume the lead—to be a *do*-er. Immediately, you may think of many men who are passive. For these men, passivity can be a means not of leading but of control or manipulation—what is known as *passive-aggressive* behavior. This trait often emerges in a man when his confidence has been badly shaken, or when his masculine self-image was wounded at an early age. Recognizing and understanding passive-aggressive reactions will allow a wife to more effectively minister to her husband and to survive the intense frustration of life with a man who withdraws because he is unsure of himself.

There are two parts to handling the problem of a withdrawn man. The first is to commit yourself to the process of helping him emerge into his God-given role, and the second is to build for yourself a strong relationship with the Lord from which to draw strength while the emerging process is working.

How does a wife enter into the process of helping her "withdrawn man" come out of himself? The first part of her task is to build the skill of "active listening."

Most of us assume that communication involves talking, but it also requires listening and looking. Women are notoriously good listeners—at least during courtship. But many times, this crucial skill is lost and forgotten after marriage.

True listening involves far more than waiting to talk. It involves picking up clues in an attempt to understand the reasons *behind* what is said and what is left unsaid. Often, a wife is at a loss for what to say to a husband who is silent. Many ask, in frustration, "How do you listen to a stone?" You don't. But neither do you try to forcefully penetrate a stone by talking at it. A wife can, however, show her husband that she cares what he's going through. And this can be done non-verbally in as many creative ways as you can imagine.

She can approach her silent husband, who has slouched in an easy chair, with a snack and the evening newspaper. She can stand quietly beside him, rub his neck and communicate without speaking "I love you. You've come to the right place after a tough day." This can work in reverse, too. Instead of *telling* her stone-silent mate about all the pressures of her day—which will likely drive him deeper into removed silence and the wife deeper into frustration—she can try this: "Honey, I've had a rough day. Would you massage my shoulders and help me relax?" If you cannot get a listening ear, you can at least have the comfort of his warm, relaxing touch.

Many women wrongly assume that their withdrawn man is so confident in himself that he simply clams up because he doesn't need her at all. This is often a very wrong assumption. In fact, he may be withdrawn because he has had his confidence shaken, has seen his dreams shattered, or has spent his day feeling defeated. As a result, he needs a safe place to go, and home should be that place.

Home has been called "the spot where when you go, they have to let you in." Many times, however, a man sees his home only as a location filled with more pressure. If he has been defeated, he is not thinking of what his wife has faced all day, nor does he see the many roles she fills. His vision shrinks to the minute size of his own life. He is left staring at the rubble of his shattered dreams. He sees his goals and his happiness slipping through his grasp.

Yes, it's true that you may have had challenges and defeats in your day, too. But the fact is, seizing your husband by the ear the moment he walks in the door is not the way to gain his eager attention. If you learn the approach of active listening, however, you are more likely, later, to get the attention you need as well.

What do you listen for?

What Is He Running From?

The desire to escape pain is a tremendous motivator for many men. For a man, one of the greatest sources of inner pain is the lack of success or outright failure.

Recently, in an interview on a news program, the race-car driver Danny Sullivan was asked, "When you're in that car, what do you fear most?" You might reasonably expect him to reply, "A crash," or "A fire." But no. Like many men would, he said, "Failure. I cannot stand to lose!"

Even men who have a strong belief in God are not immune from this male trait.

The prophet Elijah might be an example of a man who experienced depression and a paralysis of will because of a failure. In 1 Kings 18, we read that Elijah defeated the prophets of Baal. But at a time when one might expect this great man of God to be on top of the world, he made one mistake: He ran when his life was threatened.

We read that "he went a day's journey into the wilderness, and came and sat down under a juniper tree; and he requested for himself that he might die. He said, 'It is enough; now, O Lord, take my life, for I am not better than my fathers' " (1 Kings 19:4).

Elijah's standards were high, and because he had perhaps betrayed his own goals he saw himself as just an ordinary person. James 5:17 agrees and says he had a nature like ordinary men—and that included a knee-jerk reaction to run from the pain of failure. A Christian woman may think that her husband's beliefs should erase his human, masculine weaknesses. But given an event that shakes his confidence, a man's first response will be to escape pain just like Elijah.

Unlike the prophet of old, the Christian husband has a wife and family who, hopefully, are committed to seeing him overcome human weakness.

How grateful I am that I had the love, tenderness, support

and faith of my family when I was in the midst of just such a personal crisis.

When I graduated from seminary I was, seemingly, a man who was destined for success. I'd had years of encouraging ministry with a Christian campus organization, the Navigators. While at seminary, I'd been elected student body president and gained the esteem and recognition of my peers and professors. My dream was to be the pastor of a large and influential church. I was not prepared to handle failure.

My very first pastorate was with a small church suffering from financial problems. I quickly determined that a certain group of people was responsible for these problems, and in my desire to succeed, I saw these folks as obstacles. I was blinded to the fact that those "obstacles" were, in fact, the focus of my ministry. So I handled these people with terrible insensitivity and quickly became unpopular with them. One result was that it destroyed my dream of being the "dynamic church leader." For the first time, I saw my hopes for the future and the purposes to which I had given my life swirl down the drain. I felt like a colossal flop.

My reaction was to withdraw and go through the motions of life with one thought in mind: *Avoid further pain whenever possible.* The change in me was so pronounced that even my children noticed.

During a particularly depressing series of church board meetings, I'd go home each evening and lose myself in the world of television fantasy. That same week, I'd committed myself to working on a model plane with my son Joel, then six. As we sat down at the kitchen table to work one evening, I switched on the TV. We worked, but I paid little attention to Joel. After some time of receiving only mumbles and grunts in reply to his many questions, he finally turned to me and said, "Dad, is the TV your best friend?" To add conviction to injury, my six-year-old went on to say, "You know, Dad, Jesus is my best friend."

I sat there stunned. My son's insight went far deeper than he could even imagine. He recognized my need for a friend to distract me, someone on whom I could lavish time and attention—and that someone, at the moment, was a mechanical box.

In the end, it was the love and attention my family poured out on me that brought me out on the other side.

Lashing Out

There can also be another side to the withdrawn man. When he is not immersed in silence, he may be demanding and critical. Having lost the battle in his working world, he may turn his attention to the one place he still seeks to prove his dominance—his own home.

One of the obvious first signs is that he will become less and less considerate. He will contribute little effort to help with the chores that make the household function. When his wife points out his shortcomings as a husband, a father and a Christian, and the more she communicates a lack of respect for him, the sooner he will decide that home is just another place filled with hard knocks. This produces a downward spiral with results that can be devastating.

Another sign that a man feels his failure has thrown his life "out of control" is that he will take on only "safe" tasks. Why should he attempt something that carries with it the uncertainty of risk? Therefore, some men will pull back from activities over which they don't maintain a high degree of control, or in which they aren't certain of success.

I saw this happen with Tom when he lost his job. Though he did not admit it at first, it was a terrible defeat.

Now, Tom was also a good auto mechanic. He had an aged car that he tinkered with as a hobby. With a cavalier attitude, he told Cindy, his wife, "Now I've got the chance to put that old convertible back on the road. I'll look for a job when I'm ready. So don't bug me about it."

Tom told his friends he had enough money saved so that he could take his time to pick the job he wanted. He even bragged that he might make so much money on the sale of that old car that he could start working for himself. In point of fact, he was spending more cash for parts than their situation allowed, and he knew he was only staying busy enough to allow himself the luxury of not thinking.

Only later did Tom admit he was really afraid of being

turned down for a new job. He deeply feared that his own incompetence or personality had cost him his former position, and he had no desire to suffer through a series of job-interview rejections.

The more Cindy expressed fears for their future, the more Tom heard one theme loud and clear: "You're not providing for us and you're a failure." Cindy never said it, but Tom heard it. When Cindy initiated prayer, urged Tom in Bible reading or some area of spiritual leadership, he only saw her dissatisfaction with him. Whenever he entered the house and heard Cindy talking on the phone to a friend from church, he could tell by the hushed tone of her voice that he was the subject of conversation. He dreaded the glances of her friends at church and was embarrassed when the pastor inquired if they needed help. Therefore, he continued to lose himself in car grease, matinee movies and Monday Night Football.

To compound his inner doubts, Tom began to see that his circumstances were putting him in the same place as his own father, a man who had never held a steady job for long. That notion horrified and angered him. He had no desire to live a life where he lacked respect. Tom became suspended between the fear of being a second-class citizen in his own home and his need to avoid the risk of further failure.

It was only after Cindy began the process of expressing her trust in Tom again and the belief that he would do the right thing that he began to see his home as a place where he could be safe. Home for Tom became a location where he could be understood and an avenue where he could risk failure and still not be devastated.

Each day Cindy's smile told him she believed in him and simply chose to ignore his failures. With that encouragement, Tom's inner motivation grew. Cindy's attitude toward her husband was not one that came from a down-trodden self-image, but one that was a deliberate choice on her part. Her favorite phrase and the subject of her prayer life became: "It's God's job to change my husband, and it's my job to love him."

The complexity of today's world often freezes people, like Tom, between choices. When a man finds himself at a crossroad in life, he may believe it is actually *wise* not to act at all. He then becomes glued in his tracks to indecision. In his desire to do the best thing for himself, and the perfect thing for his dreams, he does nothing. If he is still employed in a job he dislikes, he may remain so, in the desire to wait for the perfect moment to switch. Meanwhile, his dissatisfaction and emotional withdrawal from his family continues.

The actions—and more importantly, the *reactions*—of a woman whose husband is undergoing a crisis are critical. It doesn't help to say, "My husband knows the Lord. Why doesn't he just pray?" The facts are that Christ has given each of us a ministry, and the wife may be the only expression of God's love that her husband can see during his most trying times!*

Now, I'm not suggesting that a woman should overlook or ignore her own needs when trying to help her husband out of a time of emotional withdrawal. In fact, while she is learning to listen and to wisely communicate her love in practical ways, she must not neglect her own emotional and spiritual needs. Only by learning to press on in her relationship with the Lord will a woman be able to handle her own pain, which will merely compound the marital stress if allowed to churn out in negative words and reactions. The path to helping her husband and, therefore, *ultimately helping herself*, starts with her own walk with the Lord.

The Path to Peace

Often a woman marries believing her deepest needs will be met in the relationship with her husband and in the family and home that promises to be hers. There is that tendency in each of us, men and women alike, to view our spouse as someone predesigned to meet our own needs. But only God himself can satisfy the longings of our heart.

In his book *Men in Midlife Crisis*, Jim Conway offers encouragement to any wife who is undernourished emotionally because her husband is going through a major crisis. He emphasizes: "The sense of worth must come from *within* the woman. . . . She must say, 'I am worthwhile; I am valuable,

---

*There are times that call for a woman to draw a firm line and push her husband into adult behavior and away from his need for mother love. (More on that in chapter 7.)

not because of what I do (and not because of who shows me attention), but because I am God's creation—because I am me.' "[1]

When a husband's focus has dwindled to the sum of his own hurts, any woman will begin to doubt her worth as a person. Conway goes on to underscore: "There is a depth of self-esteem within a woman's personality that cannot be touched by what other human beings think. *Only God can meet her deepest needs.*"[2] (Emphasis added.)

A woman's walk with God can start with a simple morning devotion—a time where she comes before the Lord to spend a few quiet minutes reading the Bible and asking Him to speak to her spirit.

As she feeds her soul regularly in this way, the voice of God will begin to have a greater influence on her than the absence of her husband's voice. As the love of Christ speaks to her daily in Scripture, the lack of her husband's love can stop dominating her reactions.

Another step to finding a solid platform of peace is for a wife to learn how to develop a different view of her husband.

By that I mean that strength and peace also come as you view your husband not as he is at this moment, but for what he is going to become. That long view of life must dominate a woman's prayers and thinking. This perspective is like the confidence that Christ shows in each of us. He sees all that we are, but He also knows what we are destined to be.

I find a wealth of encouragement in reading about the incident wherein Jesus revealed Peter's soon-coming betrayal. In Luke 22:31–32, He says, "Simon, Simon, behold, Satan has demanded *permission* to sift you like wheat; but I have prayed for you, that your faith may not fail; and you, *when once you have turned again, strengthen your brothers.*" Jesus' focus was not on what Peter was—a soon-to-be coward—but on what he was to *become.*

In 1 Thess. 5:14–15, Paul gives a list of how we are to treat each other. He tells us to ". . . admonish the unruly, encourage the fainthearted, help the weak, *be patient with all men.* See

[1]Jim Conway, *Men in Midlife Crisis* (Elgin, Ill.: David C. Cook), 172.
[2]Ibid., 173.

that no one repays another with evil for evil, but always seek after that which is good for one another and for all men."

If we merely react to what irritates us in our spouse's behavior, we will find ourselves doing the opposite of what we should—*encouraging* the unruly and *admonishing* the fainthearted. The natural thing a woman all too often does with a husband who is dominating or behaves childishly is to quietly give in to his "unruly" behavior. The tendency she also has with a man who is discouraged and in pain is to comfort him. Both of these knee-jerk reactions are the exact opposite of his real needs. In one case we invite being stepped on, and in the other we kill the patient. In the case of the husband who has passively withdrawn, the wife must have the wisdom of Christ to know her husband.

Admittedly, treating someone with love when he is acting in a self-centered, *un*loving manner is humanly impossible. And that is precisely why a wife must daily place her trust in Christ and rely on Him for strength.

Build His Hope

Every slot machine in Las Vegas fills up with coins because of one principle: People play them and may finally lose everything, but they'll continue to play until the bitter end if they have hope of eventually winning. The gambling casinos make sure there are periodic "payouts" in order to keep customers throwing in their coins. *Unlike* the gambler, the withdrawn man is living his life in the expectation of a negative payout. He is convinced that underneath everything, he is a failure. Each and every disappointment becomes a periodic reminder of his negative presupposition. Therefore the safest thing for him to do is to simply stop trying. He firmly resists putting good effort down the drain. For the man who has emotionally withdrawn, the hope that burned in him years before may now be no more than a spark that he seeks to protect at all costs. He wants to live out the rest of life as painlessly as possible. But there is limited joy now and few prospects for it in the future. He may believe that he has blown his one big chance in life and it will never come again. If a wife is to have a major impact, she must ask God for the wisdom to help her to focus her husband on *hope*.

There are several creative ways she can work on this task.

1. Begin to keep a prayer diary of little things she is praying for in her devotional time. Keeping track of the ways God is answering prayer will also build hope.

2. Acknowledge that even the things her husband is now doing to avoid responsibility as having potential *future* value. (For instance, Cindy could say to Tom, "You're such a great mechanic. It makes me feel safe to drive around in a car I know you're looking after.")

3. Find something he has done in the past that is paying off now. Compliment him. ("I'm grateful you built that barbecue. We're getting so much good use out of it this summer.")

If these simple steps are undertaken and continued patiently as a ministry, a wife may show her husband that she believes in his future and his worth, even if he does not. This can be done without sounding "preachy." And more importantly, she needs to be involved in encouraging her husband in a way that will give her hope as well.

Build His Confidence

A person lost in the morass of his own discomfort can still do something well, even if it is only to clean his plate! Shifting the pendulum from what he is *not* doing to what he is managing to do will scent the atmosphere of his life with newfound confidence.

Begin by waiting to catch him doing something right. Few things are as irritating as having to step around a husband who has become a "couch potato." Almost everything he does, which may be very little, is grating to the nerves. Then the small things that he may do are quickly overlooked, with the thought, "He should have done that a long time ago."

Include as part of your personal prayer list this daily request: "Lord, let me catch him doing something *right* today— *anything*!" Thanking him for his smallest deed as soon as possible can be a positive reinforcement.

As newfound confidence develops, your husband will be a happier man to live with.

Remember That First Date

When marriage is filled with more withdrawals than deposits, it's easy to forget why you married in the first place. How many women torment themselves with the question, "What did I ever see in him?"

Some time ago, a former neighbor who is an unbeliever approached me on a ticklish subject. He told me he was having an affair. He told me he'd decided that his wife no longer met his needs and that their relationship was totally unsatisfying.

After hearing him out, I asked, "What is there about your wife that first attracted you to her?"

He mulled over the choices and gave me quite a list. "She was attractive! Intelligent. I enjoyed talking to her. She is organized—a great manager. And she's a fine woman."

I asked, "Have any of those qualities changed?"

After some thoughtful silence he replied, "No, I guess they haven't." Looking right into his eyes, I said, *"Hold that thought."*

Some time later, I was outside washing my car when he stopped by and told me that he had ended his affair and had a renewed interest in his marriage. As he left he turned to me and said, "You know, that's the best thing anybody ever did for me—telling me to focus on her good points. Where did you get that idea from?"

You and I both know where that idea comes from—1 Cor. 13:8, "love never fails. . . ." The same love that drew us to our mates so that we wanted to spend our lives with them is still there. It may be covered over with the trauma of irritations and the loss of romance, but it's there, nevertheless.

Of course there are other ways a husband may withdraw from his wife and family. He may not have experienced the blows of failure or hopelessness. It may be that he has given his emotional energy to pursuits outside the marriage, like sports, or a hobby, or a group of "buddies."

One of the most widespread problems today, in our culture that has become so success-oriented, is the problem of "workaholism." Commonly, we think of the workaholic as the man who stays on the job from sunup to sundown, including weekends and holidays. We think of him as someone who is relatively successful, though he may not think of himself that way. But a man may have other obsessions stemming from his work that are not so readily noticeable.

In the following chapter, we will face the challenges of living with the man who is wedded to another activity—his work.

To youth, I have but three words of counsel—
work, work, work.

—Bismarck

6

The Workaholic

Lumping the man who is addicted to work in the category of a passive husband requires a degree of explanation. A man who is passive at home is not necessarily so in other areas of his life. The woman who lives with a busy man who never gives *her* his attention is bewildered as to the place she holds in his life. She may assume that she is unimportant in his life, or that he doesn't love her. In point of fact, he is merely being a man—but a man who is busy staying out of touch with his own feelings and those of others.

In *The Workaholic and His Family*, a consortium of Christian counselors write: "A workaholic is anyone (including the housewife) who uses busyness to avoid getting in touch with personal feelings, to stay clear of intimacy, or to feel adequate or significant. . . . [He] is generally a very nice individual, especially in the eyes of a society sold on the Protestant work ethic."[1]

To make money and to provide for family are only partial explanations for why men work. They seldom play a part, however, in reasons why men *overwork*. When you listen to men introduce themselves at a social gathering, it's unlikely that you will hear, "I'm John, and I make $22 an hour." But they

[1]Frank B. Minrith et al., *The Workaholic and His Family: An Inside Look* (Grand Rapids: Baker Book House, 1981), 49.

will identify themselves by job title, or use their company's name—especially if it denotes status. Studs Terkel, in the preface to his book *Working* describes work as "a search for daily meaning as well as daily bread."[2]

In his book *The Secrets That Men Keep*, Dr. Ken Druck gives a summary list of reasons why men work. He highlights the following:

- We work to express who we are. ("I'm somebody; this is what I do.")
- We work to have a purpose for living.
- We work to feel "a part of something greater" than ourself.
- We work because the act of working is intrinsically satisfying.
- We work to achieve social improvement.
- We work to leave our mark on humanity.[3]

These are all wonderfully valid reasons for getting up morning by morning and fighting the traffic on our way to spend time with strangers whom we greet as comrades-at-arms in the work force. These reasons seem more commendable than simply punching a time clock and saving for a new sofa. In fact, when a man approaches work with a balanced lifestyle and the rationale listed by Dr. Druck, a wife will greet a happier, more fulfilled husband when he returns home at night.

But the workaholic is not balanced, and that is the problem. He lives a life that is obsessive. He usually experiences frustration that characterizes his life in general. Work, therefore, becomes the only place where he can "blow off steam." It may be one of the only places where he can receive the strokes he so desperately seeks. He may also believe he's a loser in life, and this, too, will contribute to his compulsive need to prove himself at work.

Most women find that their efforts at correcting this self-destructive course drive him further away into the arms of his "corporate mistress."

[2]Studs Terkel, *Working* (New York: Pantheon Press, 1974).
[3]Dr. Ken Druck, *The Secrets That Men Keep* (Garden City, N.Y.: Doubleday & Co., 1985), 133–134.

"Grief, anxiety, feelings of rejection, unfulfilled sexual excitement, guilt, depression and hostility can be warded off by plunging into work," says Jay B. Rohrlich, who practices psychiatry on Wall Street. In his book *Work and Love: The Crucial Balance*, he adds: "The old story about the man humiliated by his boss who comes home and beats his wife is far less common than the opposite: the man frustrated at home who goes to the office and 'attacks' his work."[4]

Druck lists reasons why a man empties himself into his work. He calls these, "Secrets men hide in the workplace." Though a man may not even know he is acting on these inner reasons, they shape his actions nonetheless. In summary, the reasons are:

- Work becomes one more hiding place for our feelings.
- Work becomes a hiding place for our fear of failure.
- We use our work as an excuse not to live more fully in other areas.
- We work to hide a sense of personal inadequacy as men.
- We work as an indirect expression of love for others, ("breadwinner's love").
- Work becomes a hiding place for feelings of aggressive competition with fathers, older brothers, former classmates and business rivals.[5]

When we recall the building blocks that produce uninvolved husbands and the essential differences in the way a man views his world (that his ego and self-worth are built outside of the home), it's easier to see why a man loses himself at the office. It's a mistake to assume that overwork shows a lack of love for the Lord or his family.

Let's consider the major reasons why a man gets lost in the world of work.

A deep sense of inferiority.
Men who are consumed with work are occasionally confronted by co-workers who ask, "What are you trying to

---

[4]Jay B. Rohrlich, *Work and Love: The Crucial Balance* (New York: Summitt Books).
[5]Dr. Ken Druck, op. cit., 134–136.

prove?" In fact, they may have *much* to prove. A man may come from a home where enough was never enough.

In seminary, for instance, I knew a number of grown men, with families, who faithfully copied their report cards to mail them home to Mom and Dad. One told me his most vivid memory of his father was being told, "You'll never make it. You'll never be good enough." In his desire to become a pastor, I'm sure he never thought that a church selection committee would ask him for his GPA. But for him, grades had become a litmus test of self-worth.

An individual who overworks because he feels inferior and needs to climb to the extraordinarily high ground of his own standards will always be late coming home from the office. Because he believes that what he does is never good enough, he cannot bring himself to accept that the *quality* of his life is most important. So he buys into the wrong notion that *quantity* will cover up for a lack of quality. But we are rarely rewarded because of how much we've accomplished.

Norman Wright, in his book *Understanding the Man in Your Life*, writes about how men and women approach the subject of vocation from a distinctly different direction:

> Women take more of a pragmatic approach to work. They see employment as a means to an end. Most everything in a man's world is connected to his work. If you were to ask a woman who she is, she would probably respond with a number of terms describing her relationship with the world and the people around her. Not so with a man. He will probably reply with a list of what he does and what he owns. This could include his house, car clubs, associations, titles, duties, responsibilities and hobbies. A man's work is the way he can attain all of these items.[6]

Paul reminds us of how our lives are evaluated by God. In 1 Cor. 3:13, he shows us a picture of our final examination by God:

> Each man's work will become evident; for the day

---

[6]Norman Wright, *Understanding the Man in Your Life* (Waco, Tex.: Word Books, 1987), 173.

will show it, because it is to be revealed with fire; and the fire itself will test the quality of each man's work.

If God himself is to test the quality of our lives, no amount of "cramming the night before" will allow us to rise to the top of the class. Unfortunately, the workaholic's standard for his own life is different than God's—and harsher. He cannot pass his own test and his "self-talk" tells him he must never let up on his quest to accomplish more and more.

False guilt.

Doug was a friend of mine who never saw himself as "good enough." He had an older brother who was bigger and better in every area that counted when they were boys. He also had a younger sister who was smarter and seemed "cuter." So he grew up seeing himself as "not worthy of attention" and feeling that he lacked any valid way of gaining approval. When he brought home his report card, his dad would say, "Good— two A's. But what about this B in spelling? I thought we taught you better than that. You know George (Doug's brother) never has any problems with spelling. Why do you?"

False guilt never lets you up off the wrestling mat. When your finished tasks never meet with approval, you begin to assume that *nothing* you do is ever good enough. As a man, there is a nagging feeling that "this won't do—I just don't think the boss will be happy." If you ask a reason for this opinion, the reply is, "Just a gut feeling." And the grave dilemma is that this feeling never goes away on its own.

The workaholic has grown so accustomed to never being satisfied with his own efforts that he actually demands a greater volume of accomplishment just to feel safe in walking away from the job. He views any person who asks him to stop his work either as competition or as someone who wants him to fail, or someone who doesn't understand his standards or the complexity of his job. The truth is, not even *he* understands his standards.

The obsessive, driven personality.

Gene had the highest standards of almost anyone I ever knew. He went beyond the boundaries of reasonableness in almost everything he did. While carrying a full schedule of collegiate teaching, he pursued a seemingly endless quest for his Ph.D. He had begun his own business, was making major renovations on his house, taught Sunday school, sang in the choir and was in training for a marathon. If you asked him why this lifestyle was necessary, he'd give you "air-tight" logic for programming each ten-minute interval of his day. The arguments alone would leave you out of breath.

Not content with merely *attempting* these immortal feats, he had to attain a high degree of excellence in every one of them. In order to have enough time to prepare his lessons and study for his classes, he'd rise around 3 A.M. to burn the predawn oil. In order to do this, of course, he had to retire before his wife and children, but they understood. . . . After supposedly studying until 6, he would run—not a leisurely jog, but a break-neck time trial, trying to better his time from the previous day. His time at home was time spent with a hammer in hand, or with a bookkeeping ledger open, or on the telephone pushing his business—doing all of this while trying very hard to maintain the picture of the perfect Christian husband and father. I listened to his wife remark one evening, "Gene's a wonderful father, but the children always ask, 'Can't we ever do anything right for Dad?' "

Someone who maintains this pace seldom receives our compassion. But had you known Gene as a youngster, you would have seen a very sensitive boy. Even in a household of eleven, he was singled out for a spanking almost every day (that's right) of his boyhood. He didn't have cruel parents. But they were Christian disciplinarians who were determined to raise a perfect son. They instilled in him the virtue of discipline. So much so that when he had to go to the bathroom at night, he'd lie awake "holding it," knowing that if the creaking floor woke his parents, he'd be spanked. Inside of "Gene the college professor," he was still that frightened little boy, lying awake in the dark, trying with all his might to do more than should ever have been expected.

In *More Communication Keys for Your Marriage*, Norman Wright discusses the perfectionist:

A perfectionist probably received parental messages

which included: "You can do better"; "That's not good enough"; "Always do better than others"; "You'll receive love if you perform"; "Beat the next guy." We remember comments, words, withheld praise, double messages, sad faces, frowns, signs of disappointment, requests for more this, more that. And so the treadmill of striving is perpetuated. The perfectionist has an endless goal of pleasing his parents. They may no longer be around, but their parental message is still a recurring childhood memory.[7]

When the obsessively driven person insists on maintaining a life of toil, he is not indicating his lack of love for his wife or his lack of reverence for the Lord. He is indicating his lack of love for himself and the firm belief that nothing under his care will ever be good enough. By necessity, he has become a preoccupied man who is distant from his family and no amount of guilt from his wife will help.

Wrong values.
To the workaholic, the workplace provides him with an arena in which he can realize his inappropriate goals. Promotions are an available barometer of success. The shiny new car in the parking lot is seen by co-workers, and the accumulation of things have a way of eventually being posted for all to recognize. Everyone in the office knows who comes out first.

Like the compulsive personality, the man with wrong values is unsure of how worthwhile he actually is. He has been led to believe that he can prove his worth by a striking financial portfolio and a nice house filled with expensive things. His standard of achievement is based on the ever-changing values of others and that of actors mouthing advertisements. It is to this individual that the German race-car salesman speaks when he pitches his "iron roller skate": "You deserve a car like this. You've earned it." A man is left to wonder, "If I don't have a car like this one, does it mean I don't deserve it?"

---

[7]Norman Wright, *More Communication Keys for Your Marriage* (Ventura, Calif.: Regal Books, 1983), 59.

Druck shares the story of Jim Sanderson, who writes a column for the *Los Angeles Times*, entitled "The Liberated Male," which is circulated by over 200 newspapers. This is his story, as he confessed it to 10 million readers.

Millions of men are still obsessed with the idea of "making it" or "being somebody." You always start with the idea that you'll work harder (and be smarter) than the next guy. You work long hours and never sleep much. Your mind is always churning up new ideas, battle plans and competitive fears. It's a relief to leap out of bed and get moving each morning. You don't have to like your work; you just have to be good at it. Moving up in the world is all that counts.

Some mornings I'd get to work so early I'd pass the hookers coming in from a long night in midtown. At times I'd think that maybe deep down we were a lot alike—they sold themselves for money at night; I sold myself during the day.

But there were good times as well—the euphoria of pitching a new account and winning, of pushing our gross up another notch, of making our little company noticed in the industry. Sometimes the good feelings would last for a couple of days . . . or a couple of martinis.

But in the end there was always that nagging feeling that I wasn't moving fast enough. Every setback so savagely depressed me that the only answer was to work harder. I spent such long hours in the office that I never saw my kids awake. I would sneak into their bedrooms at night with a tiny flashlight to look at their sleeping faces and reassure myself that they were still alive.

Some dim voice of conscience pleaded with me to get out of this kind of life. But I always rationalized, "I've come this far. I can't go back now."

When you hear the words "push, push, push" pounding inside you like a giant heartbeat, when you don't have the time to play with your kids, to spend an evening making love, to rejoice or commiserate with a friend, then you certainly do not have any generous emotion to spend on a stranger. Art? Music? Reading for pleasure? What's the "bottom line" in all of that? Where's the "payoff" in the real world?

Needless to say, I was not a good husband during that time of my life.

"What is it that you really want?" my wife cried in desperation one night.

"A million bucks," I told her.

"Then what will you do?" she wanted to know.

"I'll start living," I replied with no hesitation at all.

Some men have to have a heart attack before they realize they must change or lose everything. For me it was the shocked look on my wife's face. She didn't say anything as she stood across from me. There are moments, horrifying epiphanies, where no words are needed.

In the end it was not as hard to get out of the business and find a new career as I had thought. I've spent several years now rediscovering the real world. I've done a lot of searching back, too, to try to learn when and why I decided material success was worth paying any cost to achieve.

Life is so short and precarious that we are fools if we do not constantly examine the meaning of our harried days. Few people are ever satisfied with their success, no matter how grand. You never really "make it," because your goals keep reaching ahead of you. And if in trying you lose love and your humanity, then you've lost it all.[8]

"For what will a man be profited, if he gains the whole world, and forfeits his soul? Or what will a man give in exchange for his soul?" (Matt. 16:26). As believers, we see our souls as already saved and concern ourselves with other matters. It is difficult for us to see that the soul is far more than a vessel for the afterlife, that it is also a temple of worship and a rich jewel God is polishing to show in this life.

The desire to avoid confrontation.

Men love competition; it's *confrontation* they hate. Men see confrontation as a win/lose proposition. And most husbands

---

[8]Jim Sanderson, "The Liberated Male," *Sun Features, Inc.* Used by permission.

have no desire to make their wife the loser. After all, they reason, "I've got to live with her." Yet, they have even less desire to lose themselves. They may spend the entire day avoiding situations that reflect poorly on their competence and have no intention of coming home to a wife who makes them feel incompetent as a husband or father.

For a man, the weight of facing a disgruntled or disappointed woman is the last thing they want to bear after a long day. If he already sees himself as an incompetent because he carries a parental verdict about his imperfections, or if he watches a peer climb past him on the ladder of success, he will do whatever he can to avoid the pain of added disappointment.

Even a Christian husband—one who has a degree of sensitivity about his spiritual leadership in the home and his accountability for the emotional welfare of his family—can see his walk up the driveway to his wife as a "no win" situation. It is for that reason that many may simply put more and more effort into the one area they believe they can change the quickest—their work.

A mind set on the project, not the process.

Few men take the time or energy to attend to details. They try to see the big picture and move from point to point on the horizon of their lives, with seldom a care about the beauty or ugliness of the journey. A man tells himself that where he is going is so important that the price he is paying to get there is worth it. Generally speaking, men are *project-oriented*. A woman who is married to a project-oriented man can feel like another one of her husband's projects—some "thing" that he scribbled on his "to-do list" while he was single.

When Tom was courting Cindy, they always prayed together. They spent long hours going for walks, talking about their lives and what they both thought and felt. Tom seemed so romantic and filled with careful observations about Cindy's needs and desires. He always asked her what she wanted and made every effort to please her. Tom was such a personification of Prince Charming, that his abrupt change of behavior after the wedding convinced Cindy that she had married a self-serving person who cared little for her, and worse, someone whose motives she could not trust.

The same Tom who became the crushed and withdrawn man that we saw in the previous chapter had become a confirmed and driven workaholic. The changes Cindy saw in his life had been startling. In all of his moods and life changes, Tom was still that little boy filled with self-doubt, armed with all the wrong answers about what it took to be a man. For the workaholic, the answer to that question is found in the compulsive need to accomplish things by means of his own superhuman efforts. He does not look for it in others and his relationships with them, and he doesn't even look for it in his relationship with God. To him, the Christian life is one more set of things to do. He is never content or satisfied with what he has done.

Tom began to change only after he clearly saw that his pain was not solved by moods of withdrawal or through periods of compulsive work, but in his understanding of what God asked him to be as a man. That change came about only by accepting life as it is—including it's disappointments—and by refusing to believe that those small glittering fleshly accomplishments that men use to prove manhood had anything to do with God's view of masculinity.

There is a third type of male passivity at home. It is just as driven and frantic as the workaholic. Yet, this person sees the solutions to his needs not in hard work, but as a magical act of fantasy or play. His comfort is the white knight of fantasy and the magic wand of escapism. In the next chapter, we will chart his perilous course.

I can't think about that now. I'll go crazy if I do. I'll think about it tomorrow.

—Scarlet O'Hara in
Gone With The Wind

7

The Escapist

Many contemporary writers have brought the escapist male to our attention and, unfortunately, have struck a responsive chord in a huge segment of women in America. This note is widely recognized: It's the toot of the horn from a sports car that can't be paid for; the beep of a video game in the lap of a forty-year-old; the rustle of the "movies-tunes" section of the newspaper in the frantic search for something that hasn't been viewed a half-dozen times.

Escapism is the terminal quest for fantasy and pleasure, the emotional drugs that deaden the pain of defeat and allow one more day of avoiding the sense of disrespect. Having fun has always been a fascination for the escapist. It's part of what made dating this man so much fun and living with him an unstructured, romantic experience. However, many women who are married to escapist husbands soon notice that the romance becomes self-directed and the fun has the bittersweet sting of reality waiting at the end.

Dr. Dan Kiley, in his national bestseller *The Peter Pan Syndrome*, calls this person a "man-child" who refuses to grow up. He writes:

> The man wants your love; the child wants your pity. The man yearns to be close; the child is afraid to be touched. If you look past his pride, you'll see his vul-

91

nerability. If you defy his boldness, you'll feel his fear. . . . Look to your children or the child of a friend and ask yourself: "What would happen if his body grew up but his mind didn't?"

This man-child is the victim of a serious affliction. If he is not helped, his life will slowly turn sour. He is not mentally ill, nor is he incapable of functioning in society. He is, however, very sad. He sees life as a waste of time. He tries hard to camouflage his sadness with gaiety and sporting fun. Often his trickery works, at least for a few years. Eventually, the people who love him become discouraged with his immaturity. Their disappointment seems unwarranted and their disgust a bit premature. But once you see what they see, you understand their wish to be rid of this person.[1]

"This Is Not My Fault!"

The hallmark of the man-child is his chronic irresponsibility. This has become the watchword of how he lives, day-in, day-out. Occasionally, the pressures of events he cannot alter bring change. In fact, his habit of putting things off invites the adrenalin-rush that he thrives on and the surge of emotion he needs in order to get the things done. Most men would simply rely on self-discipline. But he knows he's not most men. So he has simply resigned himself to his fanciful escapes from reality or the never-ending hope that someone or something will simply come along and rescue him.

Throughout this chapter, I want to trace the story of Jane and her husband, Eric, who was one of those men-children. Eric was like a big kid—in fact, that's what Jane called him: "The big kid." He held down a job, but couldn't remember to take out the trash or turn off the burner on the stove. He always had a good excuse, one which somehow let him off the hook morally. But his habits made Jane feel as if she'd become little more than a babysitter. The problem was that this big baby wrote checks and carried credit cards, indulging himself daily.

Eric taught school, but unlike most teachers he spent most

---

[1]Dr. Dan Kiley, *The Peter Pan Syndrome* (New York: Avon Books, 1983), 3–4.

afternoons at the shopping mall or in the matinee. He would take up new hobbies and disappear in the newfound pleasure until he tired of it. He devoted himself to racket ball for hours every afternoon. Jane would return from a full day, clean up his breakfast dishes, do the laundry, prepare dinner and set the table. Eric would return with his gym bag (usually late) with a new excuse about why he didn't (he used the word *couldn't*) take out the garbage in the morning. This went on for months.

Everyone liked him. He was the life of the party—every party he could find! Jane said, "Eric simply can't turn down an invitation to a good time. If he knows something is going on with his friends or the guys at the church, he can't bear to pass it up." Eric's faithfulness at these functions was viewed as commitment, but only because the pastors at church couldn't see the unpaid bills, dirty cars, messy desk, pile of garbage, uncut grass and unmet family needs that he left in the wake of his pleasure cruise. Sooner or later the effects of this mentality catch up with the person. It caught up with Eric at home when Jane decided she could take no more. And it caught up with him at his work as a teacher when a new principal saw through his good nature to his lack of preparation and the slip-shod appearance of his room.

Rooted in the desire to avoid responsibility is the need to give it to someone else. For years, Eric avoided confronting his repeated failures by blaming others. He labeled Jane's concerns as her "stressed out" reaction to a new job. He believed that the new boss had singled him out for special, negative treatment. "He wants to put a muzzle on Christians," he told me. Even when confronted with the problem, Eric admitted that he made mistakes—then in the same breath laid the fault at his mother's doorstep. "She never thought I did anything wrong." Unfortunately for Jane, she increasingly found herself in the role of "mother." And, an even greater tragedy from Eric's perspective, it was a role she was no longer willing to play.

Confusion About Adult Love

The escapist is a romantic. It's one of the things that attract people to him. He feels that he loves other people deeply, yet it is a love based predominantly on feelings. While the "work-aholic" believes he is expressing love when he goes to work and buys his family things, the escapist rarely attempts to prove his love by what he does. Responsibility is the missing dimension.

It is this immaturity that allows the escapist to look deeply into his wife's eyes and swear his undying love for her—and at the same time refuse to pick up his underwear or pay the bills on time. He's learned to receive practical, adult-type love. But he's never had much practice at giving it. Yet 1 John 3:18 tells us: "Little children, let us not love with word or with tongue, but in deed and truth."

Halfheartedness

If an activity can't be classified as "play," then the escapist will only approach it with halfhearted interest at best. Halfheartedness becomes a convenient escape from account-ability. He can say, "If I fail, it's because I don't try hard enough."

In Eric's life, it was easy, at first, to miss his lack of effort. He began to mask his withdrawal by developing a desire for another career. He was convinced that his summer job as a waiter or his hobby of watercolor painting might blossom into something to remove him from teaching—which he now de-meaned as "glorified baby-sitting." These mental relief valves prevented him from facing his need to put all of his effort into life today. They formed the centerpiece of his wishful thinking.

An "Abracadabra" Mentality

For the escapist, fantasy is fatal. In children, you expect and encourage creative thinking, and to some degree it is also healthy in adults. But for the escapist, it becomes a reason for inactivity and irresponsibility. He actually believes that some-one or something will come along to his rescue. He is sure that his fantasy will slay every difficulty, not with hard work or discipline, but with a mystic happening outside of the realm of work or responsibility.

He dreams about inventing the new kitchen gadget, winning the multi-million dollar lottery or writing the great novel that will put him on Easy Street. He knows that if he keeps dabbling with his paints, someone will discover him and make him famous. And he sees instant money in his dream of owning his own company, never realizing the amount of work that goes into running a business. Emotionally, he is still that little boy who doesn't know where money comes from.

Somehow this adult male came to believe that love should mean unconditional support and be that magic wand waved over every problem to make it go away. The problem is his boss doesn't like (love) him. His wife doesn't understand the pressures he faces (love him). That magic wand of love that he has always waved at his problems doesn't work anymore. But, that won't stop him from waving it. His real problems are rooted in self-respect. He has little or none. And in his realistic moments he is consumed with painful self-doubts—doubts that in the past have always been waved away by the wand of love.

Procrastination

The life of the escapist is marked by chronic procrastination. His self-discipline is very poor and the habit patterns etched into his character make him avoid anything that brings pain or discomfort. The escapist has lived a life of finding his way around difficulties. Sometimes his experience tells him that the best way around a problem is just to sit still. If he says, "Just a minute, sweetheart, I'll get to it in a bit," he knows that his wife will become impatient and do it herself. He lives for the moment, and when he finishes savoring his moment, there will always be time for work, preferably later.

Dr. Dan Kiley, in his book *The Peter Pan Syndrome*, writes on the subject of procrastination:

> The Peter Pan Syndrome victim's procrastination is much more devastating than the kind you and I occasionally indulge in. We put things off for a day or two because we are tired, our mental energy is sapped, or we just can't find the time. But we *will* get it done.

The PPS victim most likely will *not* get it done. He puts things off because he has little if any reason to invest himself in tomorrow. He figures that any energy spent will only result in more failure. This fatalism turns ordinary procrastination into disaster. Things are *always* put off until tomorrow. Obviously, they never get done.[2]

There is a type of emotional high to be gained from waiting until the last possible moment. The escapist male receives a sense of satisfaction from seeing other people race around in a loving attempt to pull his life out of the fire. This magic wand of love, accompanied by a plea for pity, has often worked in the past. People actually jumped into the fire to show how much they cared about him. In becoming a spectator to this exercise, he continues to believe that love—or what to him is love—will continue to rescue him. What he doesn't see is that each successful rescue only spells his further doom. The escapist is a taker—a nice taker, a bright taker, perhaps a Christian taker, but a taker nonetheless.

Eric felt a deep love for Jane, yet he had grown up never understanding that love carried with it the mandate of action. When the stress of their marriage became unmanageable, Eric viewed it as a lack of love—that is, a lack of Jane's love! "Sure, I've got problems," he'd say, "but if she'd just accept me the way I am and really love me, I know things would get better."

Because the escapist can be so charming, so giving of emotional love, the wife of the escapist can easily think, *I must be doing something terribly wrong to cause him to act this way.* On many occasions, Jane's confrontations with Eric were followed by his pouting and sulking in an attempt to play upon her mothering instincts. Jane's guilt and her further resolve to understand and love Eric were unfortunately followed by Eric's repeated patterns of overspending, procrastination, self-indulgence, and irresponsibility.

---

[2]Kiley, *The Peter Pan Syndrome,* 79.

How to Help Him Without Becoming His Mother

To help someone caught in the quicksand of escapism takes not only patience and love but the wisdom not to fall into the morass yourself. There are a number of classic wrong responses that women use in dealing with a passive/preoccupied husband. (These will be detailed in chs. 7–9.) For now we will limit ourselves to some do's and don'ts and to some strategy for dealing with the escapist.

Norman Wright has counseled scores of couples enmeshed in these escapist problems. He highlights several responses a woman should avoid in dealing with the dilemma:

> Don't let denial become a part of your life. Denial is saying, "This is not happening to me. He is not this way." How does denial express itself? You excuse his behavior with alibis, ignore his selfishness, dismiss the feeling that something is wrong, or keep reminding yourself how much you care for this man even though he treats you atrociously. You inconvenience yourself, pick up his clutter for him, write him notes so that he won't forget and try to hide those items he should have remembered. Denial is dangerous since it may spread to other areas in your life as well. Allowing a man to continue to act as a child does not help him, nor does it really show love toward him. Denial can hide your own pain from you and make you vulnerable to the approaches of another man.[3]

Denial is the attribute of an overprotective mother. This is precisely the role that the escapist's wife should avoid. It is the type of adult-child love that is very confusing to him and breeds further irresponsibility. Overprotective mothers are also prone to complain compulsively and to punish a misbehaving child only randomly. The child grown-up is accustomed to these reactions and has some well-rehearsed reflexes. He simply ignores repeated complaints and uses the guilt in

---

[3]Norman Wright, *Understanding the Man in Your Life* (Waco, Tex.: Word Books, 1987), 181–182.

anyone who tries to punish him to manipulate pity from them.

When complaints move from the private to the public arena, the resentment that is built in an embarrassed man may solidify his determination never to accommodate his wife on the issue of her repeated criticism. To him, to do so would be to surrender his masculinity for the world to see. It would also admit that the self-doubt he carries around is indeed accurate. Wright goes on to discuss this complaining:

> Complaining soon moves into another response, which elevates the woman into the position of judge. You become an expert on this man. And if a man goes along with your judgments and changes for a time, you are now in the role of a puppeteer pulling the strings and—once again—mothering. You become the expert by telling the man how he feels, what his behavior means to him, what he is really thinking. When telling (not asking) him to do things, you give the instruction in such a way a kindergarten child could do it.[4]

People quite naturally live up to the expectations aimed at them. The man who is treated like a grade-schooler and who has grown accustomed to the strings attached to him by his manipulator can comfortably settle into a life of no-change sameness. He is free to develop a natural excuse and a convenient place to fix the blame for his lack of effort. The best his wife can expect is a return to the old patterns of unresponsiveness. The worst she can dread is a deep resentful anger toward her as his female "Professor Henry Higgins." In the end, her husband will be persistently looking for someone else to show him the tenderness he believes he will not receive at home.

For many years, I've worked in ministry to single adults. It always amazes me how much time, effort, and tears go into the process of finding just the right life partner. And yet, invariably, when someone finds "the one," he or she wants to change that person. This is sterling testimony either to our incredibly poor insight into people or our lack of knowledge as to what we want. Knowing our mistakes in past judgment,

---

[4]Wright, *Understanding the Man in Your Life*, 182–183.

how can we be sure we now know what we want? We also must come to grips with the reason for an intense desire to change our partner. What are our objectives?

The Trauma of Change

Men gravitate to routine. The inertia of behavior for a man is a dominant fact of life. Often I will hear wives complain that when they go out to a restaurant, their husbands will inevitably order the same thing. Oh, they may take a long time to look over the menu, but in the end it's steak, as always.

That is because to their husband's mind, that restaurant has come to mean one thing—"steak." A change of choice for him will involve either a change of dining rooms or a polite waitress who will tell him, "I'm very sorry, sir, but we're out of that this evening." Jane simply stepped into Eric's life and politely told him, "I'm very sorry, sir, but you'll have to take out the garbage and pay your own bills."

In a group of twenty-five couples, all in an adult Bible class, I asked the question, "When you change anything in your life, what makes you change?" Of the twenty-five men, eighteen listed a crisis or some similar upheaval. While I wasn't surprised at the numbers, I was surprised at the honesty of the notes on the questionnaires.

A selection of response cards read like this:

- A crisis usually makes me act when there is something that needs change. A family argument, total frustration, or strong emotional outbursts usually indicate the need for change.
- Circumstances such as the loss of a job, traffic accident, etc. I'm very adaptable.
- Usually I'm shamed into it, or nagged to the point of anger.

But the nail was hit by another anonymous husband who penned these words:

- A major painful crisis with my back against the wall; *or* when the pain of change is less than the pain of the situation.

Passive Resistance

For a wife who has grown accustomed to it, refusing to "mother" can be painful. Some women may be faced with the disturbing thought that perhaps this role was exactly what they wanted in marriage. They saw the escapist's irresponsible tendencies, and they felt right at home with the prospect. The challenge of taking someone and remaking him might have been an equally compelling reason. Whatever the rationale, the notion of now opposing this lifestyle by doing nothing goes against all of her natural instincts, including her *maternal* desires.

Eric's habit patterns included giving no help around the house. To Jane it was a constant source of irritation. He sat watching TV while she asked, "Could you take out the garbage?" Her second, third, and fourth requests were always fended off with his desire to wait for a commercial, to finish the article he was reading, or the excuse that he had to wait till morning when he could see.

When she'd finally had enough, Jane agreed to begin some passive resistance. She asked Eric the familiar question, "Would you take out the garbage?" She asked only once. Thereafter, she began filling paper sacks beside the overflowing garbage can. The children noticed their shrinking kitchen, but it took Eric five days and walking into the pile on his way to the refrigerator between commercials to bring up the subject.

Jane's reaction was a calm one: "I asked you to take that out the other day. I knew you'd get to it whenever you were able." It was a polite but firm reply that communicated esteem for Eric and a new line that she would not cross. There are easier ways to handle a garbage problem. But Eric and Jane's problem was not garbage; it was irresponsibility.

Jane found pleasure in controlling her emotions by refusing to become angry. She also noticed a new delight in not allowing her emotions to be dictated by her husband. Her confidence grew to the point that she told Eric, "Sweetheart, you can notice when the garbage is full. From now on, I'll just let you decide when to take it out." Basically, Jane had to decide what she could live with—an overflowing trash can, or a growing anger and resentment toward her husband.

The difficult area for Jane was the checkbook. When they both agreed on a budget, it was decided that Eric would pay the bills. She got a check each week for groceries and her areas of management, i.e., clothes for her and the kids, school supplies, and household expenses.

Jane knew it was only a matter of time before things would bog down financially.

Several months later, as Eric looked for socks among the discards scattered across the top of his desk, he noticed and dug through the overdue bills piled around the "IN" box—just where he and Jane had agreed they would be placed. Frantically, he ripped them open to survey the damage. Each one was more devastating than the last. They were like cold buckets of water on a groggy morning. As he came down the stairs to find Jane, he felt angry and inwardly frightened.

Jane tried not to blink as he screamed into her face. She calmly looked into his eyes and said, "You agreed to be in charge of our finances, sweetheart. I did put the bills where you told me."

"Why didn't you open them and tell me about them?" he shouted.

"I just thought of them as your mail and I had confidence in you that you'd take care of them," she responded.

Later, as a much calmer Eric talked to me, he reassembled his thoughts. "I knew that all my life I just tried to get by. I didn't think of myself as lazy, but I suppose I was. I know I wasn't God's prize husband. Jane deserved better. But that day it hit me. *Things weren't going to get any better if I didn't change.*"

What Jane had been trying to get across to Eric for twelve years, the garbage can and the bill collectors had managed to perform in three months!

In a marriage, three things can change: The wife, her mate, and their relationship. A woman can decide to change at least two of those three. Any movement in her own life *will* change their relationship. If she changes, he must make adjustments in response to her.

In the final analysis, when it comes to dealing with the escapist, a woman has two choices. She can enter into his avoidance-fantasy pattern with him, or she can keep herself healthy and move toward more wholeness. Though she will undoubtedly face struggle, recriminations and perhaps even childish manipulation, her greatest chance for saving her husband and her marriage lies in holding on to reality with both hands.

For this woman, the promise of Jesus himself must surely offer great encouragement: "For you shall know the truth, and the truth shall set you free" (John 8:32).

For since he would sit on a Prophet's seat,
As lord of the human soul,
We must needs scan him from head to feet,
Were it but for a wart or a mole.

—Tennyson, "The Dead Prophet"

8

A Portrait of the Man David

In Sunday school classes all over the world, children scramble for crayons and try to stay "inside the lines" while they color pictures of the marvelous shepherd boy named David. Crouched in small circles, they listen with shining eyes as their teachers tell them how their hero faced the giant Goliath, and was victorious. They dream about what it must have been like to stand with that young warrior. Never in a million years do most of those children imagine that David could do anything wrong. It's easy for them to keep that illusion, because a Sunday-school teacher is telling the story, not David's wife or one of his own children.

David, surprisingly enough, is a good example of a passive and preoccupied husband. I base my conclusion on several important factors: We know many of the intimate details of his family life, including enough information about his home to know that he was, in many respects, a distant husband; yet, we know that he was still classified a "man of God." These factors do not seem to agree with each other; however, they describe one and the same person.

Many a Christian woman enters into marriage with the mistaken notion that all she needs for happiness is a man who

105

shares her doctrine. Later, she can be appalled at the predicament she finds herself in—married to a man who loves the Lord but does not know how to love *her*. The answer is not that her husband needs more piety or doctrine, but that they both need to understand how God made them and how He intended them to work and live together.

The notion that our spiritual heros might be deficient as husbands or fathers is a concept foreign to us. Ours is an age of high-gloss media, polluted by the illusion of flawlessness. The very notion that a spiritual hero could be troubled by family problems seems a contradiction in terms. It's hard to believe that we could sit in the pew and listen in rapture to a preacher who, forty-five minutes earlier, was yelling at his wife and kids from behind the Sunday morning paper. But the men who inspire us are just folks, not super human cover boys for *Christianity Today*. The real men and women we are married to have the ability to be godly and yet irritate us at the same time.

David is proof that a man can make serious mistakes—and still be respected by people and used by God. Looking into his family life and into the background that produced his behavior patterns has, in fact, caused my respect for him to grow. But more important, it has magnified my respect for the grace of God. It's humbling to consider the poor material God chooses to work with and, to me, it glorifies His skill as a master builder of people.

David's Boyhood Home

Home *is* the formative place. There we learn who we are, what the world around us is like, who God is, and how to make our way in life. We make important starts in lifelong habits at home.

We can't accurately describe David's home in its architecture or give a completely vivid historical account. But we know that the only model David had to look back to for the answers to the crucial questions of his own personal life was the home of his father Jesse, in Bethlehem of Judea.

The factors young David confronted there and how he responded to them are what built into him habit patterns that he would later display as an adult. The same factors David faced are timeless.

Low Self-esteem

While we don't know the type of discipline David received, we can get some sense of the esteem he was given. In 1 Samuel 16, we read about the visit of the prophet Samuel to David's home. This was in all likelihood the proudest day that the household of Jesse had ever experienced. A visit to their home by Israel's great prophet of God. David was the only person absent. This absence was no oversight. Everyone knew where David was: he was keeping the sheep. That alone was an indication of David's status.

Being the family shepherd was not the choice job. Shepherd's work was dangerous. David himself talked about the dangers when he recounted his experience with the lion and the bear (1 Sam. 17:34–36). A shepherd was also somewhat of a social outcast. He smelled like sheep! In contrast, we can consider Joseph, a younger son who was his father Jacob's favorite. In Joseph's home it was the older boys who were given the shepherding task, while he was kept at home for more seemly duties (Gen. 37:4, 12–13).

In addition to having the dirtiest job, David was the missing man. Even after Samuel's mission was revealed—to find Israel's next king!—the old prophet had to prod Jesse into bringing forth his eighth son, young David. One can only wonder to what extent David grew up feeling like an afterthought in his own house. It's quite likely that David always got the "short straw."

Home is meant to be a place of value and love, spiritual treasures that come to us from the mind and heart of God, and which He asks us as parents to pass on to our children. It is this godly, sane and healthy view of the inner self that will form the good habit patterns of a lifetime. A sense of security and significance will affect how our children respond to work, to the circumstances of life, to God himself and to other people.

In our work with the Navigators, over the years my wife and I have had many people come to live in our home as part of our ministry with college students and post-graduate singles. One such young lady, Maggie, lived with us for the better part of a year prior to her marriage. During that time, we discovered that she was constantly uncomfortable around me.

We talked about it many times, but it always boiled down to the unspoken sense that I was unhappy with her behavior around the house, or with her ministry on campus. Neither of these feelings was accurate. Yet, even after much time spent assuring her of my support, love and gratitude for her efforts, it was a feeling that she couldn't shake.

I began to feel that, perhaps, in some way I was communicating these attitudes—until the week before her wedding, when I met her parents and grandparents. They were highly critical people. I realized that what she felt in our home was what she expected to feel throughout her life. There had simply never been a time when she didn't feel unworthy, incapable and undeserving of praise.

Moreover, her father's form of discipline was to give her the "cold shoulder" whenever she did something he didn't like. She would remain in this "frozen" state indefinitely until her father spoke again, letting her know she had done enough to make amends for her misdeed. Sometimes, though, she never even knew what she'd done wrong.

During the week, I even received some advice from him on the discipline of my children. "Never spank them," he said. "I never did. I just stared at them." I smiled at him and listened politely. But what cold looks and "cold shoulders" do to children is far more damaging to their self-esteem than any spanking could ever be.

Faith in a Personal and Loving God

David's home may have had flaws, but its greatest strength was its faith. As a shepherd boy, David turned to his own faith and to prayers, which cultivated his walk with God in the lonely fields while tending his father's sheep.

Dr. James Dobson, in his book *Hide, or Seek?*, writes:

I believe the most valuable contribution a parent can make to his child is to instill in him a genuine faith in God. What greater ego satisfaction could there be than knowing that the Creator of the Universe is acquainted with me personally? This is self-esteem at its richest, not dependant on the whims of birth or social judgment, or the cult of the superchild, but on divine decree.[1]

A Lack of Individual Attention

Each child has a need to be a significant and unique human being—not just a member of a group, but a special person. He should not have to compete with other members of the family for love and recognition. To remind our own children of how much they are loved, my wife and I used to sing a special song to them at bedtime, or if they'd been hurt:

> When Jesus sent you to us,
> We loved you from the start.
> You were just a bit of sunshine,
> From heaven to our hearts.
> Not just another baby,
> For since the world began,
> He's had something very special
> For you in His plan.
> That's why He made you special,
> You're the only one of your kind.
> God gave you a body and a fine, healthy mind.
> He has a special purpose that He wants you to find,
> That's why He made you special,
> You're the only one of your kind.[2]

The message that comes through loud and clear when we treat our children as something special and significant is that they are loved. That love is not based on some ideal image of them, but on the perspective that recognizes differences and still says, "That's just the way we like it around here. You don't

[1]Dr. James Dobson, *Hide, or Seek?* (Old Tappen, N.Y.: Revell, 1974), 156.
[2]"You're Something Special" by William J. and Gloria Gaither, © Copyright 1974 by William J. Gaither. All rights reserved. Used by permission.

need to be bigger or thinner or smarter or more athletic to be our child. Jesus gave us *you*! And we're happy about that."

Unfortunately, many parents have an "ideal role" already assigned to a baby at birth—one which God never designed for that child. In David's case, it is plain to see that not only was Jesse raising him to be a shepherd, but he was not open to the possibility that David could be king. Samuel had to wait while each of David's older brothers was paraded before him. Then he turned to Jesse to ask, "Are these all the children?" Jesse replied, "There remains yet the youngest, and behold he is tending the sheep" (1 Sam. 16:11). Until that moment, Jesse had apparently never even considered David as anything but his "shepherd in training."

Children are a quick study of their parents. If they need to be different to gain approval, they'll know that, often before the parents are conscious of it.

Joel was born to us the year after I stopped coaching high school football. No one needed to tell him I was a fan and would be delighted if he decided to play football. The crib he was placed in when he came home from the hospital was lined with the decals of all the teams of the National Football League. A small, blue plastic football was his first toy. Being a graduate of the University of Washington myself, Joel's first word was "Husky," our team name—which I taught him. Therefore, even as a toddler, Joel knew he could always get my instant attention by the simple act of picking up that blue football. When he lobbed that oblong ball in the air, I'd stop whatever I was doing and he would get a round of applause.

I have since discovered, though, that the boy I had pictured as a linebacker is musically and artistically inclined, with very little interest in sports. I have also discovered that God's plan is much better than mine, and I have learned how to cooperate with that plan.

Home Is a Place to Be *Away* From

The normal reaction of any child who is at the wrong end of a parent's favoritism, or who is being forced to live up to a wrong ideal is to become defensive and "difficult." They do it by withdrawal and isolation, or by acting on the urge to prove everybody wrong. And what better way to prove the world wrong than by setting it on its ear? Achievement, too, is a wonderful revenge. It is this need to achieve and prove oneself that often becomes the fuel for the workaholic husband and passive father.

To David's credit, he not only accepted the negative aspects of his upbringing, but the rejection he must have felt as a youngster also gave him a tender heart. The isolation and danger he found in caring for a flock of sheep in the wilderness helped create an ability to commune with and trust God. Not every young man responds positively, though, to being shut out emotionally at home.

When a child grows up in a home where he is ignored, there are several factors that make becoming an active husband and father an upstream proposition. First is the lesson that was communicated: "Home doesn't meet my needs." Because home didn't help me in the past, it stands to reason that it will continue to work against me when I have one of my own. We build a home, using the blueprints we discovered in our own childhood homes. The feeling of unhappiness a boy experienced when he walked across the threshold of his boyhood home continues to trouble him when he comes home from the office years later as a husband and father.

There is also the notion that if happiness can't be found in family relationships, then other people or things *will* satisfy the desires we have for stimulation and ego satisfaction. The idea that "what I need as a man is found outside the family" is learned at an early age. The "castles" every man feels he must build in life become things like jobs, power, prestige, money—anything but the home he actually lives in. Like many up-and-coming executives, David's home most likely taught him that what he really wanted in life was to be found someplace else.

Sibling Rivalry

David's home was not unlike other homes in the fact that there was a great deal of rivalry among the children. As one of eight boys, he must have been involved in constant warfare. Children are often like opposing generals, testing their opponent's weaknesses so that, at the right moment, they can launch an all-out attack to bring about destruction.

Observe the story of David when he decides to fight Goliath. On hearing the giant's boast, David asked, "What will be done for the man who kills this Philistine?" (1 Sam. 17:26). Listen to the ensuing attack from his oldest brother, Eliab.

Eliab's first challenge was this: "Why have you come down? And with whom have you left those few sheep in the wilderness? I know your insolence and the wickedness of your heart; for you have come down in order to see the battle" (vv. 28–29). Note the sarcasm and the judgmental attitude.

Sibling rivalry has a great deal of bearing on the drive to succeed. It also carries with it some weighty emotional baggage. First, it is motivated by the need to prove your worth. Second, your personal goals are often wrapped up in the need for revenge against another member of the family. It also fragments a family unit, scattering the members in the direction of their own ego-gratification so that it is impossible to enjoy another member's success. Finally, it reinforces the idea that a person's worth cannot be promoted in the family unless it's at the expense of the others.

In fact, much of what we promote in our Western culture is competition at the expense of other people. Parents who themselves are crippled by this need to compete are usually incapable of helping their children overcome it.

Even the idea of murder came from the first family of the Bible. When Cain killed his brother, Abel, it was in a fit of jealous rage. A sense of competition, in which he had been the loser, built up in Cain until he took it out violently on the person he saw as the favorite, his brother. It's been estimated that if we could reduce anger in the home, we could cut violent crime by half.

Stopping the War

How do we defuse the time bomb of sibling rivalry?

A good place to start would be to change the attitude of

parents. Is there something that we, as parents, are out to prove in life? To whom? As a football coach, I faced many a father who was living out his dream of a career as an athletic champion through his son.

Another factor that contributes to sibling rivalry is parental fatigue. The fact is, we're just too tired to get involved with the petty struggles of our children, not realizing that those struggles will not change greatly unless we do intervene. They may, however, be twisted and later come out in more "socially acceptable" forms.

Many times I have seen church leaders exert heavy-handed influence on unsuspecting congregations. A man or woman like this will often stop at nothing, including splitting the church, just to win a point. What their parents thought of as a temporary phase that they would outgrow has now become a dangerous and desperate need to dominate others.

Third, parents need to maintain authority over the home, including a child's attitude. Attitudes of hatred and rage that go unexpressed should never be ignored by the parent. Waiting until habitual emotional sparring becomes a knock-down, drag-out fight is losing the war.

Another important goal is to make the expression of love a full family enterprise. There is nothing wrong with developing a family that enjoys telling each other how much they love one another. In our own home when the kid's bury the hatchet, they don't just apologize, they hug and kiss. As a family, make it a practice to regularly talk about why you love each other.

Criticism and Expectations

Let's return to David's conversation with his older brother, which also displays two other common family traits: criticism and the power of expectations.

Eliab wrapped himself in the robe of one who "knows all." Looking down his nose at his little brother in verse 28 of 1 Samuel 17, he said, "I know your insolence and the wickedness of your heart." That you know someone's heart is a heady claim to make, but we often do it. When a youngster makes a natural mistake, it's too easy to blurt out, "That was a stupid thing to do." These kinds of sweeping decrees go into the fiber of a young personality because they pass judgment on the child's inner being. Likewise, high expectations are imprinted on the young soul as well.

Criticism and expectation each represent one half of the mold that a child is poured into, because young children grow up believing that the parent or older sibling possesses some mystical knowledge concerning their life or future.

In particular, a parent's inability to see his children in a realistic light will vividly promote a lack of self-esteem. If we communicate a shortage of faith in them, their own aspirations will most certainly be low. If, on the other hand, our expectations are sky high, the child's first failure can result in a crash of confidence.

The net result of parental or authoritative input is that we try to live up to the expectations that are voiced concerning us. When "all-knowing" adults, older brothers and sisters, laugh at a youngster's expense, we may call it good-natured humor; but that's a one-way perspective. We tend to think that a child's ego it too small to damage. But the pain they experience is real. The impact is far greater because of how much of their world we adults represent.

The young boy who grows up in a critical environment can develop the idea that not only is home an unpleasant place to be, but that he must *prove himself worthwhile, no matter what it takes or who it hurts.* This is the perfect training for a passive husband and father. He becomes the guy who claws himself to the top, only to crawl home and lose himself in four beers and Monday Night Football.

Is There Hope?

There most definitely *is* hope! You can't turn back the clock, but you can reset the hands and wind it up again. Great changes can be made by stopping the cycle of criticism. The following are some things to keep in mind.

Start by expressing confidence in your child and your mate.
I started into the primary grades with a well-deserved reputation for being a "holy terror." I don't remember many

weeks in the first or second grades when I didn't have to stay after school. My penmanship excelled because of the consistent after-hour chalkboard writing I did.

But then the most significant day of my schooling came, the day I was pushed out of the second grade and came to know my third-grade teacher, Mrs. Smith. She had gray hair and wore it in a bun in the back of her head. Today, that hairdo and her black dress and black buckled shoes would make her look like someone directly out of Hollywood central casting with a sign marked "teacher."

During that first day of school she had us work quietly while she went from desk to desk to speak to each child. When she got to my desk she said, "So you're James Walker."

I nodded.

"I've heard so much about you, James."

I thought, *I'll bet you have.*

Then, surprisingly, she looked through my eyes and into my little soul and said, "And I don't believe a word of it!"

It was then that I knew I'd found someone who believed in me, a life-changing experience that caused me to dedicate my year to proving that *she* was right!

Know the ages and stages of the people you love.

We parents have such a great compulsion to see children as little adults. Childhood is not a punishable offense. Discipline should be carefully administered for willfulness, not childishness!

Recently, the story came out about a teacher who failed all of her second-grade pupils. Her reason: They were "immature"! It seemed that these eight-year-olds couldn't sit perfectly still and listen to her lecture for forty minutes each day. Someone should have told her that while she was telling them to sit still, their own natures were saying "Wiggle!"

It pays to know the life stages that your mate is facing. While many people have been critical of mid-life-syndrome books, who can fault anything that teaches us to be better observers of our mates and more sensitive to the pressures they face? We're each confronted with the dilemma of allowing our own needs and desires to drown out the cries for help being given out by our loved ones. *"Me first"* is the battle cry of the sin nature in each one of us.

Know the tendencies and singular qualities of the people in your household.

It takes time to know people and accurately assess the talents and potential achievements of each one. It also takes an approach dedicated to building your child's self-image. Why spend years trying to develop a talent that will never be there to your satisfaction when there are other God-given abilities lying fallow for want of attention? If God in His wisdom has given you a concert pianist, quit trying to make that child into a hockey player! We also need to aspire to high spiritual ideals for our children and carefully balance what is and what is not possible.

Years ago, Walt Disney coined a new word—"imagineering." Walt did not look for the engineer who restricted his thinking to what his blue pencil and calculator said was possible; he looked for the man or woman who dreamed big dreams and then proceeded to make those dreams happen. There must be a little of the "imagineer" in each parent.

Know what your expectations are and where you got them.

It's important to decide if you're being unrealistic in your expectations for others. It might be a good step to find out what those expectations are. Many times, critical thoughts we express to our children are merely a product of *not thinking* ourselves. We don't know what we want.

After finding out what we want our children to be, a second step would be to find out how we ever got such a notion. Does it come from our own unfulfilled dreams? Is it because we went through the great depression or suffered from unemployment that we want our children to have financial security at all costs? Or is it because we had a bad day and it's just easier to yell at the children than to kick the dog?

Create emotional "trail markers" for our loved ones' lives.

Make some indelible impressions on the lives of your family members. How much more pleasant it would have been if

Eliab had encouraged David rather than undercut him in front of the other soldiers.

Keep a scrapbook for your children, with pleasure-filled milestones. These don't have to be press clippings or star-studded reviews. They can be as simple as a letter. Try not to give just birthday presents, but letters and prayers that express your highest hopes and dreams—not just for their status in life but their character and their joy. The toys will break and the cards will be lost, but those hopes of yours will go on and on.

Be a Role Model

The importance of having someone to pattern your life after is never more critical than in the home. This is perhaps an area in which our Western society and its fast-paced times have provided the greatest havoc in the home. As sons watch Dad leave for work—or, more likely, find him long-gone in order to beat the traffic—what do they learn about the role of husbands and fathers in life? Because they see Dad build his life around things outside the home, they can think that is what it means to be a man. In too many cases, the *absence* of a model becomes the model.

David fits this dimension reasonably well. But he was also a victim of what, for him, was poor role-modeling. His father Jesse was more of a grandfather figure to David than a father. We're told in 1 Sam. 17:12 that "Jesse was old in the days of Saul, advanced in years among men." This showed David a father who could no longer take a very active part in the life of the family, or bear significant responsibility for the discipline and modeling of his children. In short, Jesse was, of necessity, a passive husband and father in the eyes of his young, impressionable son David.

This vacuum of leadership was readily filled by David's brothers. You can rest assured that it will be filled in the homes today, too. It will be filled by teachers, rock stars, TV heros and, most likely, mothers. The result will be that the modeling process will go on, but the image on future generations will not be a pretty one.

An Undutiful Daughter will prove
An Unmanageable Wife.

—*Benjamin Franklin,*
Poor Richard's Almanac, *1752*

118

9

Abigail, the Doormat With Lace

We are told that in marriage "two shall become one." Our problem is *which one?*

The struggle for personal identity in marriage can easily become an undercover brawl. Frequently, after the luster of a new marriage and the excitement of the honeymoon has worn thin, one partner or the other silently asks, *Can I be the real me and still stay married to you?* If the answer to the question is *no*, the wife may choose to hide her "real" thoughts, desires, and personality. A Christian woman may actually believe that in doing so—in nearly erasing herself—she is living the biblical lifestyle of the submissive wife.

Assertive Submission

True submission is a deliberate and thoughtful act. It is born of choice, not necessity. We are told to have the same attitude that Jesus displayed. Philippians 2 tells us, "He emptied himself . . ." (v. 7) and "He humbled himself . . ." (v. 8). These were deliberate and carefully thought through actions that Christ did *to himself*, not the knee-jerk responses of a man who saw himself as inadequate.

119

Keeping the delicate balance of submitting our own desires to the will of God and, as a result, subordinating satisfaction to the needs of those around us should be the attitude of every believer, not just the married woman. When Paul instructs women to "be subject" to their own husbands (Eph. 5:21), he prefaces his remarks by saying, "Be subject to one another in the fear of Christ" (v. 21). Submission is a Christian virtue, not just a mandate to women.

My wife, Joyce, does some substitute teaching. She enjoys it, but when she has had a difficult day, she comes home in need of gentleness and understanding. The best compassion I can show her is not measured by listening or talking, but by doing. I pitch in and help with dinner, setting the table, and otherwise lightening her work load. When I've had an equally stress-filled day, though, it's a temptation to just sink into a chair, watch the news and lift the newspaper to shield my eyes from her smoldering glance. What I do at that point is make a decision to submit. It is my own decision. It is also a measure of my Christian character. I have not always made the right decision, but I'm working on it.

Submitting your desires to the needs of another should be carefully thought through. It ought to be based on the legitimate needs of another and on your own determination to be like Christ. It is a choice. It is a spiritually assertive act.

Unfortunately for many men and women, submission is a habit pattern borne out of a low self-esteem. It has little to do with the direction of God. It is not based on the legitimate needs of another. It is based on the fear-fed choice to avoid pain. It can cause a marriage to deteriorate, not grow, because it increases hostility and bitterness. God is intensely interested in the *reasons* for our actions.

We see an illustration of this in the story of David. He was a man of God. But as that title might indicate, he was a man. We would be hard pressed to find one with more promise who became a greater failure as a husband and father. The reactions of three of his wives display the most typical responses of women to a husband who is much less than promised when he comes home.

At first glance, most people view Abigail as a humble heroine, and that is likely true of her. But if we examine her from the perspective of our own culture, we may reach some different conclusions. Now that may not be fair, but in the light of how we view such situations today, we might say this about her:

Her self-image was rooted in her status, not her own qualities.
Historically, a little girl in Abigail's day was not highly esteemed. Her birth was lightly regarded. Being a form of household servant, her father was expected to pay a dowry to someone, anyone, who would take her off his hands. She had little choice in most instances and could only hope for the best and grit her teeth while the deal for her husband was settled. Not knowing Abigail's childhood home, she may have had the seeds of inferiority sown in her in many ways. As an adult she certainly carried about the fruit, as we will see, even though she seemed a remarkable woman at first glance.

Many women today who carry about a negative self-image have little, outwardly, to point to it. They are attractive and competent in most respects. It is almost as if they had never seen a mirror, or seen one of their report cards. We read in 1 Sam. 25:3 that Abigail "was intelligent and beautiful in appearance." Her negative self-view had little to do with her God-given qualities.

Her cold marriage was built by fear and distance.
The final episodes of Abigail's marriage are reported in 1 Samuel 25. She hears of her husband's rude and offensive behavior to the young warrior David, whose men had been protecting Nabal's herds. She responds to the news in a way I'm sure she had practiced many times before. Out of her fear and disrespect for Nabal (probably greatly deserved, I might add), she goes secretly around him. Making wide circles around this man may have been the easiest thing to do. Abigail's habits did not solve her problems and never brought any form of closeness between her and her husband. It also deprived him of the best moderating influence he had. The account in 1 Samuel 25 says, "And she said to her young men, 'Go on before me; behold, I am coming after you.' *But she did not tell her husband Nabal*" (v. 19). You have to wonder how many other times Abigail had left Nabal in the dark.

Her habit was to assume self-blame.

We find a clue to another common attribute in overly submissive women in 1 Sam. 25:23–24. Upon seeing David, we are told:

> She hurried and dismounted from her donkey, and fell on her face before David, and bowed herself to the ground. And she fell at his feet and said, *"On me alone, my lord, be the blame.* And please let your maidservant speak to you, and listen to the words of your maidservant."

Dr. Kiley in his book *The Wendy Dilemma* talks about women who continue to mother men, and discusses this trait toward self-propelled martyrdom.

> Self-blaming is a free-standing behavior, but as a precursor to self-sacrifice, I consider it part of martyrdom. The self-blamer is constantly under self-imposed duress. Her voice of inferiority causes her to cross-examine her every thought and action, hunting for blame, no matter what the situation. She says, in effect, "I'm not a good person, so I must have done something wrong. I just have to find out what it was."[1]

A woman with a negative self-image has a flimsy grasp on the real world and often lives in a make-believe one where she is the focus of attention. Largely, that focus is negative. Ten positive things may happen to her in a day, but invariably she will pick out the one negative experience to characterize that day. Catastrophes are anticipated and even expected. Though someone like this may treat disaster as a joke outwardly, inwardly, lightness has no place in her thinking. The events of life all become a part of the mosaic of disaster.

Guilt was used as a weapon.

A woman whose habit has become submissive escape has few protective weapons remaining. However, she does become proficient with those. She can and does wear guilt and martyrdom well. Claiming blame is an easy defense mechanism.

---

[1]Dr. Dan Kiley, *The Wendy Dilemma* (New York: Avon Books, 1985), 106.

A helplessness that is designed to elicit pity from men is never a pretty picture, but for many women it seems the only avenue open.

You cannot fail to sympathize with Abigail. Her position was precarious and she deserved far better. Her good qualities were obvious and must have been plain to her future husband, David. He must have felt a great deal of pity as this woman came out to him to plead for her husband, "the fool." And given the hardness of Nabal's heart, David, in his sensitivity, melted with her pleas.

Bitterness and hostility were suppressed.

Because Abigail avoided pain and confrontation, the notion of expressing her feelings to the source of her discomfort—Nabal—never occurred to her. Fear of conflict sentenced her to internalize the pain. With each hurt, Abigail and Nabal distanced themselves as marriage partners and became caught in an expanding cycle. When this occurs, the past is never allowed to become the past. It continues to smolder beneath the surface, unseen but red hot.

No one can live like this. Therefore, the logical step is to allow the pressure to escape in inappropriate ways. A wife who says things about her husband to co-workers and even to total strangers—things she would never dream of saying to her husband—will put an ever-increasing distance between them. Abigail displayed her feelings about Nabal to David and, one might imagine, to his entire company. In 1 Sam. 25:25 she says, "Please do not let my lord pay attention to this *worthless man*, Nabal, for as his name is, so is he [The name Nabal means fool.] Nabal is his name and folly is with him; but I your maidservant did not see the young men of my lord whom you sent."

This type of practiced indiscretion can easily leave someone open to the temptation of an affair. A helpless woman who needs protection and is able to confide what seems to be her innermost thoughts to a man is quite an ego boost to him. And for a woman such as Abigail, any man who will listen to her and extend tender sympathy can provide hours of fantasy. The fact that David sent for her to become his wife after the news of her husband's death should come to us as no surprise. It was a natural response for a man whose sympathies had been aroused by a woman who confided her hurts and stirred his desire to protect her.

Her circumstances changed—but her lifestyle continued.

Practice does not make perfect, but it does make permanent. Repetition is an important tool in learning. As wrong patterns of thinking are repeated, the ruts of behavior grow deeper as years go by. When submission and service are attitudes of the heart and deliberate and well-considered decisions, new events in life are occasions to grow. But for someone who has a deep inclination to react in the same pattern, new circumstances mean more practice.

In Abigail's case, when David sent word by his servants that he wanted to make her his wife, "she arose and bowed her face to the ground and said, 'Behold, your maidservant is a maid to wash the feet of my lord's servants' " (1 Sam. 25:41). You might well conclude that she was simply a humble person willing to serve the men in her life. We could speculate this— if we had not seen her disposition toward Nabal and sensed that those attitudes were part of a habit pattern that was not producing the type of inner character that God intended.

All too often, a woman wrongly concludes that if only she could change her husband, or at least his actions, then life would be rosy. This is an illusion. More often than not, God is out to change us, not our circumstances. Real hope is in the fact that we have a God that can change us.

The story of Brad and Melanie

Melanie sang in the church choir, and when you saw the worshipful gaze that sparkled with devotion, you would never suspect the extreme hatred she carried about Monday through Saturday. It was a vindictiveness enclosed in an attractive and intelligent outward appearance. As Brad would bark an order in the parking lot, she would bite her lip, drop her head and, after gathering the children, drive home to her hostile suburban world.

One day, after listening to a catalog of complaints about the inattention of her husband and how harsh and cruel he was to her and the children, I asked, "What keeps you in this marriage?" Her face relaxed, she sat back in a moment of self-disclosure and said, "My dream is that someday there will be a knock at the door. It will be a highway patrolman telling me that Brad has been killed on the freeway. That's the only thought that keeps me going." Her face relaxed just as if this was a normal fantasy.

Melanie had grown up with a father who resigned the authority of his house to her mother. He slunk home with his contribution to the monthly bills, then dutifully retired to whatever place had been assigned to him. He loved Melanie, but when she got into a dispute with her mother, he was powerless to help and protect her.

Melanie's mother barked out orders and rarely allowed herself to be warm or to let her guard down. She was the exacting taskmaster that Melanie reported to every day and swore she would one day escape from. To live with her mother, Melanie had to keep her thoughts and inner hostilities to herself. So she lived in a dream world, longing for the day she would escape. For her, marriage to Brad was that escape.

Like most escapes of fantasy, the illusion was short-lived. As we talked, I asked her to recapture the feelings she had toward Brad on their wedding day. She replied, "I knew even then that this would never work. But my aunt had flown out all the way from New York, and I just couldn't call it off. Besides, my mother never would have stood for it."

For Melanie, being a wife and mother carried with it the mantle of provider, protector, and the glue that held the family together. Brad had failed in business and now had started another. To impress his clients and potential investors, he purchased a new BMW. The house payment on their new five-bedroom home was astronomical. Stress, frustration, depression and anger poured out of Brad every night. Melanie kept busy with a day-care business and cleaning other people's homes. Brad insisted, however, that her clients couldn't be anyone they knew. Meanwhile, every Sunday their doctrine and habits dressed them and sent them off to church.

In truth, Melanie had never resolved the issues of her childhood home. The temporary feelings of relief she maintained by her suppressed hostility only caused her to brood under the surface and await a new offense from Brad, one of the children, or some unsuspecting passerby.

The Emotional Profile of a Submissive but Hostile Woman

She views herself as someone of little worth.
A negative view of oneself can launch you into a lifetime crusade to prove something: that you are of unlimited worth.
In her book *Men Who Hate Women and the Women Who Love Them*, Dr. Susan Forward writes:

> As I looked for a common denominator among the women I worked with who were the misogynistic partners, I found that *they all carried from childhood a profoundly negative view of themselves.* It was this damaged self-image, more than any other factor, that set these women up to accept abusive treatment from their partners.[2]

Children begin quite early to interpret their elders' actions or lack of action from one point of view: "What my parents say or do must somehow pivot on me and how they feel about me." A child's view of life revolves around his or her own feelings. Their practice at seeing the hurts of others is not sufficiently developed to allow them to understand that people are often locked in by their own problems, problems that were not in any way created by the child.

Therefore, if a child does not get attention and affection, he assumes there is a good reason: "There *must* be something wrong with me."

She is a perfectionist at heart.
Throughout Melanie's bustling day—dressing her children, preparing dinner, doing housework for herself and others—the tape of her childhood played in the background: "You're not good enough. You never do anything right. Your bed looks sloppy. You can do better than that." She still saw

---

[2]Dr. Susan Forward and Joan Torres, *Men Who Hate Women and the Women Who Love Them* (New York: Bantam Books, 1986), 128.

herself as that little eight-year-old girl walking home from school in a big hurry, knowing that when she opened the door, she would find a verbal barrage of failures and a list of busy-work at which she could never succeed.

With each job she attempted, the slightest detail never failed to escape her attention. Naturally, she was the one called on when anyone at the church had something to do. She was a prime candidate, never having learned to say no to others. Even when complimented on a job well done, she found success hard to tolerate. She would quickly point out several ways she could do the task better next time.

She is a workaholic by habit.

Melanie's schedule served as a type of emotional narcotic. The thought of doing something she liked to do seldom occurred to her. When I questioned the things she had planned, her reaction was defensive. "You don't understand," she said, "I've got to stay busy. I like it. When I'm scrubbing other people's floors, I don't have to think about my own problems. The harder I work, the better I feel." Busyness seemed to fill up the void of emptiness.

The woman who fits the profile of an overly submissive workaholic has in her the same root of inadequate self-worth as her workaholic male counterpart. (See ch. 6.) She believes the work she does is of little or no value. Therefore, why not make up in volume what is lacking in value? With a view of her own life that is twisted and gives little promise of change, it is a formidable task to get her to objectively see her potential in Christ.

She is a mother with protective, even smothering tendencies.

It is motherhood that brings out her few attempts at confrontation. Perhaps because she felt unprotected as a girl and emotionally still feels like that powerless child, she overprotects her own children. Even when she knows her child to be at fault, taking the blame has become a lifelong mode of existence. Watching her husband back down when she takes the blame instead of the children not only feeds her martyrdom but allows her some small, secret victory over her abusive husband.

Brad, for instance, would see a collection of toys in the hallway and begin to yell at the children. Melanie enjoyed interrupting him and saying something that both she and the children knew was not true. "I told the kids to leave those there until they finished their homework." Whereupon she beat him to the blame punch. Taking the wind out of his sails in front of the children gave her a great sense of satisfaction.

An added dilemma came when the children grew too unruly for Melanie to discipline. They knew mom would cover for them. A lifetime of living under the authority of someone who would not face reality told them that they need not face it either. Mom took all the blame for the whole household.

Her strategy is to blame herself.

Melanie lived under a self-imposed sentence of guilt. Throughout the day, she cross-examined her motives, thoughts and actions, hunting for some nerve of fault. This perpetual monologue has a powerful effect. The self-talk tape that Melanie played to accompany her life went like this:

- I'm just no good. God must be punishing me for something I did wrong, I've just got to find out what it is.
- If I just go ahead and take the blame, I won't get into another one of those horrible arguments with Brad.
- What could I have done to make my own mother dislike me?
- What have I done to make him treat me this way?
- I know I'm just too sensitive. If I could keep control of these thoughts, then I wouldn't be so depressed.

When Melanie spoke about her hurts and occasionally cried, she would even apologize for that. "I'm sorry for crying," she'd say. "I know you don't want to hear this." She not only felt responsible for causing a lifetime of pain, but would not allow herself natural emotions. To Melanie, her pain was simply an inconvenience to others.

Wishful thinking becomes her path of least resistance.

The few breaks that Melanie allowed herself were mental breaks. They were not rooted in reality. Because she saw her circumstances as impossible, it stood to reason that her solutions were also impossible. Her fairy godmother was dressed in a highway patrolman's uniform regretfully communicating Brad's demise. She knew the event was unlikely, yet the distance she felt from any real solution ironically seemed to comfort her.

For Brad, who had grown up with the view that a woman must be dominated, Melanie was "ideal." For Melanie, however, that same dream was only a continuation of her personal nightmare. And she actually believed that she deserved such treatment.

The Melanies of this society are acting out a script that they have written. The very actions that would bring change in their marriage are the things that they believe they are incapable of doing, even though, within, they are strong.

The Wheel of Misfortune

Melanie was a game player. When something went *wrong* in her life, she scored. When she came for counseling, it often became a matter of playing at being the impossible case. It was easy to get her to talk, because she desperately wanted to convince me that change was impossible. But while she talked well, she did homework assignments poorly. At times she went out of her way to sabotage what gains were made. Why? If she could show that nothing worked, that everything was beyond hope, then she could comfortably avoid confronting her problems. Change is always painful and the unknown is a frightening place to venture into. Regaining self-esteem and the ability to face irresponsible people is unknown territory.

In our sessions, there were four records that Melanie played over and over:

- My problems are too great.
- I am too weak.
- No one can help me.
- What happens if it doesn't work?

In each of these tunes, the view is entirely internal. At no time is God, His Word, or His power the focus. In Melanie's mind and practice, the Christian life was intended for heaven, not earth. Fortunately, that is not God's plan for the believer.

Know That You Are Loved

In 1 John 4:7–8, we are told: "Beloved, let us love one an-other, for love is from God; and everyone who loves is born of God and knows God. The one who does not love does not know God, for God is love."

Even as believers it is possible to live embracing two op-posite notions. One is that we belong to a God who loves us; the other is that our circumstances are meant to wound and crush us. We have so calmly divorced the spiritual side of our life from the domestic, physical, and emotional areas that we seldom wonder how to justify the discrepancy between the two.

J. I. Packer, in his wonderful book *Knowing God*, under-scores God's purpose for us:

There is a tremendous relief in knowing that His love to me is utterly realistic, based at every point on prior knowledge of the worst about me, so that no dis-covery can now disillusion Him about me, in the way I am so often disillusioned about myself, and quench His determination to bless me. There is certainly great cause for humility in the thought that He sees all the twisted things about me that my fellowmen do not see . . . and that He sees more corruption in me than that which I see in myself. . . . He wants me as His friend, and desires to be my friend, and has given His Son to die for me in order to realize this purpose.[3]

Base Your Self-Acceptance on God

A masterful lesson on acceptance is found in Hebrews, a standard that must rule our thinking about ourselves and oth-ers:

No creature of His can escape God's sight, but every-thing is bare and exposed to the eyes of Him to whom we have to give an account. (Heb. 4:13, Williams NT)

In the margin of my Bible beside this verse I have written,

---

[3]J.I. Packer, *Knowing God* (Downers Grove, Ill.: InterVarsity Press, 1973), 37.

"The jig is up!" We cannot fool God. In His sight we can be no more or no less than we truly are. Try as we might to impress Him, He sees us for what we are. God does not buy our efforts at hiding ourselves, nor does He believe the false bravado or blustering attempts at self-confidence that we put forth. As the verse all too plainly points out, we are "bare and exposed" where our Lord is concerned.

If you knew that some people in town knew all about you—that they knew the hidden thoughts and motives of your secret self—most likely, you would do everything to avoid them. The thought of being with them in a group where the knowledge they carry might be spread would be unnerving. The fear of exposure would drive you away. Yet, God's response to us is exactly the opposite.

God Wants Our Fellowship in Spite of All He Knows

> So let us continue coming with courage to the throne of God's unmerited favor to obtain His mercy and to find His spiritual strength to help us when we need it. (Heb. 4:16, Williams NT)

Many women, like Abigail and Melanie, have spent their entire lives avoiding conflict. They are fearful that contention will only expose the weakness that they are convinced they carry about with them. They have wrongly learned that weakness means vulnerability, and that vulnerability brings pain. In their early years, they needed a protective love, a love that coached them through the bumps and scrapes and was there to pick them up when they fell—a love like that of our heavenly Father. It is that "unmerited favor" the writer of Hebrews assures us we have. It is that type of love which substitutes "courage" instead of fear and pain.

It is no accident that sandwiched between verses 13 and 16 of Hebrews 4 we read:

> Since then we have in Jesus, the Son of God, a great High Priest who has gone right up to heaven itself, let us continue to keep a firm hold on our profession of

faith in Him. For we do not have a High Priest who is incapable of sympathizing with our weaknesses, but we have One who was tempted in every respect as we are and yet without committing any sin. (vv. 14–15, Williams)

We need to base our convictions about acceptance on the person and the work of Christ, and that alone. It is the work and the position of Christ that allows us to have confidence as we approach God. We gain boldness also from the fact that ours is a God who does not just coldly understand what we are going through. I like the way the King James Version puts verse 15: "For we have not an high priest which cannot be *touched with the feeling* of our infirmities. . . ." *Sympathy* is a too distant term. Our God can actually feel what we feel because He has been there.

In 1971, I stood alone on the lawn of a huge hospital complex, having just come from the deathbed of my first wife. After her death, the doctors asked me to sign some papers. I was given her wedding ring. Standing on the lawn with that ring, I felt as if I had been pushed off the edge of the world.

My throat felt as if I had swallowed a razor blade. My soul was numb. This verse was the thought that God quietly suggested. "For we have not an high priest which cannot be touched with the feeling of our infirmities. . . ." My God actually felt what I felt and cried right along with me. Our confidence in any situation comes from Christ and our relationship with Him.

Are Our Own Standards Higher Than God's?

If it is true that God sees all (and it is); if it is true that God accepts us totally because of the work of Christ (and He does), then who are we not to accept ourselves? Most often, we live our lives as if God's acceptance does not really count. The only thing that matters is what we see in the mirror or what we think we see in the eyes of our friends. God's Word is designed to change not just our theology but our thinking and our lives.

Daily Habits to Cultivate

Dealing with problems of a lifetime requires a solution that changes our total lifestyle. The cycle of growth involves insight, obedience by good habits, and accountability. It might look like this:

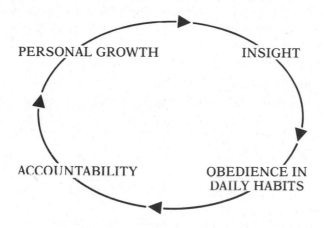

PERSONAL GROWTH   INSIGHT

ACCOUNTABILITY   OBEDIENCE IN
DAILY HABITS

The steps involved are these:

Cultivating truth in daily living.

Melanie had rarely lived according to truth. What she believed about herself was a series of lies. But as she started the day by reading Scripture, the objective truth of the Bible became a growing standard for what was true. New insights began to spring from the pages of the Bible.

One day she burst into my office. Pointing to Jer. 31:3, she read, " 'I have loved you with an everlasting love; therefore I have drawn you with lovingkindness.' "

"Can you imagine that!" she exclaimed. "God has always loved me, even when I thought no one did. Isn't that great?"

It certainly was, especially since it was her own discovery.

Learn to say no to others.

Occasionally, saying *yes* to God means saying *no* to others. The Abigails and Melanies find it difficult to say no to others. Getting the approval of other people has always been a frustration, slightly beyond their reach. The habit of stifling a no and murmuring a yes has become second nature to them. When I would see Melanie, I would ask, "Whom have you said no to today?" (Anything worth doing is worth doing daily). The more we discussed what she had been asked to do, how she really felt about what she was doing, and how she saw herself when performing the unsolicited task, the greater was her resolve. More and more she risked losing, and learned to rely on God's acceptance.

Learn to say no to self.

The overly submissive woman is herself an escapist at heart. If we were to watch her and the way she lives, we'd conclude that she says no to herself constantly. Yet, just the opposite is true. She does things for other people to gain their acceptance and to fill up the void in her life. She needs this type of approval from people far more than they need her.

The overly submissive woman can easily become a compulsive eater, drinker, or doer. The food, the drink, and the activity all help to deaden the pain of rejection and hurt. Like other compulsive personalities, what Melanie wanted *most* in life was consistently victimized by what she wanted at the moment. In her case, what she wanted at the moment was chocolate. And while she did not have a tremendous problem with weight, she had a lifelong problem with saying no to her feelings. Therefore we began to count her daily success with saying no to something she "felt" she wanted.

The results of Melanie's change of lifestyle began to surprise everyone who knew her. Not everyone was all that pleased. She could now look Brad straight in the eye when he raised his voice. She began insisting her children take responsibility. And people at the church who felt they could always call on her for work sometimes had to look elsewhere. The important thing, however, was that Melanie was far more comfortable with herself.

I knew we had turned the corner when she came to our usual Tuesday meeting and announced, "Yesterday I bought a new doormat. I took it home, sewed some frilly lace around the edges and put it out on my doorstep. Now every time I step on it, I'm reminded that I don't have to be stepped on. I can choose to serve people because God wants me to, not because I *have* to."

*When the Himalayan peasant meets the he-bear
   in his pride,
He shouts to scare the monster, who will often
   turn aside.
But the she-bear thus accosted rends the peasant
   tooth and nail.
For the female of the species is more deadly than
   the male.*

—*Kipling, "The Female of the Species"*

10

The Woman at War

A number of years ago in Newport Beach, California, a young salesman arrived at his office and while reviewing the classified ads, spotted this entry: FOR SALE: NEW PORSCHE $50. . . .

After a hurried call for directions, he steered his well-worn Ford to a well-to-do neighborhood. An elegantly dressed woman greeted him and opened the garage door to expose a gleaming, candy-apple-red Porsche. The odometer read 6,758 miles.

"Can I take it for a little spin around the block?" he asked. The woman smiled and nodded her head.

The car was a dream. The young guy wondered if the price in the paper was a misprint. Returning to the house, he was greeted by the still-smiling woman. "It looks great. But was the paper right? You want only fifty dollars?"

The lady said, "That's correct. I just had another call while you were taking your test drive."

Quickly, he wrote out the check, while she went inside to get the title and registration.

When she returned, the salesman asked the question that had been driving him crazy. "Excuse me, but why would you sell this beautiful car for fifty bucks?"

She smiled broadly and said, "It's my husband's car. Two

138

weeks ago he left town with his secretary. Yesterday, I got a letter from him telling me he was filing for divorce. He said to keep the house, but to sell the car and send him the money. So that's just what I'm doing!"

The female of the species *is* more deadly than the male.

Michal: The Rejected and Angry Wife

How can a marriage seemingly made in heaven turn into hell on earth? Couples throughout time have asked that question.

Among these were David and Michal. Theirs was a storybook romance: The beautiful princess falls in love with the handsome military hero; even the jealous king recognized the love his daughter had for the young champion and blessed their union. The society pages, had they existed then, would undoubtedly have gushed with the anticipation of David and Michal's wedding. It was a love story to end all love stories. In reading the biblical accounts of their marriage, however, we have only to turn a few pages to see how soon the honeymoon ended.

In 2 Samuel 6, we learn about David's celebration when the ark of the covenant was returned to Jerusalem. He lays aside his princely robes and romps in the middle of the parade. Whether it was because of her embarrassment at his lack of dignity, or simply because it had been a long time since he had showed anything close to enthusiasm for her, Michal displayed the brooding anger of a woman at war with her husband:

... the daughter of Saul looked out of the window and saw King David leaping and dancing before the Lord; and *she despised him in her heart.* (2 Sam. 6:16)

The dialogue that follows is quite revealing. Follow with me as we look at this couple's exchange.

Michal: "How the king of Israel distinguished himself today!" (v. 20). (Translation: "Buddy, you sure made an idiot out of yourself!")

Michal: "He uncovered himself today in the eyes of his servants' maids as one of the foolish ones shamelessly uncovers himself!" (v. 20). (Translation: "You embarrassed me by parading around in front of the lowest of the servants. You acted as if you ought to be locked up in an asylum.")

David: "It was before the Lord who chose me above your father and above all his house, to appoint me ruler over the people of the Lord, over Israel; therefore I will celebrate before the Lord" (v. 21). (Translation: "I don't really care what you think, if I'm theologically correct. Besides, God put me above your whole family, so that settles it.")

David: "And I will be more lightly esteemed than this and will be humble in my own eyes . . ." (v. 22). (Translation: "You ain't seen nothin' yet. . . .")

David: ". . . but with the maids of whom you have spoken, with them I will be distinguished" (v. 22). (Translation: "I plan to impress your female servants even more." David may have had a more suggestive point in mind when he hurled this insult at his wife.)

Verse 23 contains, for Michal, the most chilling words of all: "And Michal the daughter of Saul had no child to the day of her death." In the culture of her day the decree of childlessness was looked upon as a curse, but it may have been a simpler and more sorrowful indictment of their marriage, which entailed a cold or nonexistent physical relationship. It's quite likely that David just kept his distance from her.

What turned this marriage filled with such promise into a poisoned relationship? Some answers apply to women today, just as they applied to Michal. Any woman married to a man who is preoccupied with his own world—a world that does not include her—may quickly find herself driven wild with resentment and the gnawing sensation of being cheated. Her husband's passion, which is expended elsewhere, serves as a constant reminder that he has little appetite for her.

Even ministry and devotion to God were designed by the Creator to be *in*clusive, not *ex*clusive. A wife who is forced to go through life feeling shut out of her husband's thoughts will invariably force her way into them, and often in the only way that she feels will get his attention—by declaring war!

What Triggers Anger?

Anger lies under the surface in many women. It is allowed to brood, and when it does come to the surface it's often dismissed as a momentary lapse. "After all," a woman may reason, "when the *source* of the anger is gone, then the anger disappears." But that is not so.

Anger explodes from hidden mine fields that were planted long ago and have lain forgotten. Who placed the mine field there? Usually, one or more of the important people in our early life.

Each of us has three foundational people in our lives, people who structured for us what we look like on the inside. God has supplied us with a father, a mother, and our own inner reflective person. These three helped us early on to sort through who we are. The judgments of these three people remain buried in us for a lifetime, effecting our response to everyone else who wanders on to the hidden "mine field."

For instance, if you were told early in life that you were ugly, a hundred compliments on how good-looking you've become as an adult will never cover the hurt that remains. We focus on the negative because, deep down, we believe it.

Shadows and Ghosts

So often our self-image is haunted by two mental images. One is an idealistic self most often formed not by the Bible but by movies, beauty pageants, television, Barbie dolls or images of muscle men, not to mention unfair comparisons with others. We carry around this makeshift ideal of what we want to be, and when someone bruises that inner vision with a dose of reality, we are prone to blow up.

The second mental image is that ghost who whispers, "No way will you ever measure up to your ideal." The problem is, this ghost too is usually just a creature of our imagination based on warped ideas of what it means to be valuable as a human. We wind up being much more critical of ourselves than reality should allow, but we believe both the shadow and the ghost, struggling to live up to their conflicting demands.

We spend a lot of energy trying to prove that the fictitious, shadow-self is real. We may pour energy into becoming a success, in our playing sports, intellectualism, or flirting with the opposite sex to feel attractive. Something always comes along, however, to jab at that shadow-self.

For me the job came in the form of a simple set of car keys. In my last year at seminary, I'd become a busy boy, trying to get through a degree at a pace unknown to mortal man. I had a habit of laying things down "wherever," and that was how my car keys became the focus of one crisis after another.

I would storm around the room, shouting, "Where are my keys? Has anyone seen my keys?" Followed by the *coupe de gras, "Who moved my keys?"* In the simple act of mislaying something, I was transformed from a responsible, loving husband and father (who was studying for the ministry) into a fire-breathing monster. The children would hide, and Joyce would simply stare at the scene I was making, offering helpful suggestions on finding a proper place to put my keys every time I finished using them. Sensible suggestions were the last thing I wanted at a time like that.

Finally, I'd find my keys and drive off. But then I had to live with the thought of what I'd done. "Why," I prayed, "did I behave like a hopeless case?" I was tormented by the unchristian tirades.

What a stupid thing to do, I'd blast myself. *You call yourself a smart man, and then do a dumb thing like this! What an idiot.*

My shadow was the image of man who was totally competent at all times. I could never be late—and *never* admit to misplacing my car keys. How could I live up to this elusive dream-image and then walk in fifteen minutes late to a meeting that I myself had called! A simple set of keys had exposed for me my false assumption about myself and my demand for total competence. Whenever I went looking for my keys, that very act in itself was evidence of my inability to think. Unfortunately, when the explosions went off in my home the fall-out hurt innocent people.

Anger, to me, is one sign that the shadow-self is alive and well—even though the real-life person may not be. Anger leads to ulcers, high blood pressure, and early death. Our world is full of angry people with nowhere to get help. When I see someone lose his temper, I often find myself wondering, "What sort of shadow is he listening to?"

Several years ago, on a Sunday afternoon, I answered the phone to hear an unfamiliar voice ask, "Is this Jim Walker?"

"Yes," I replied. "Can I help you?"

"No," he answered. "I've got a shotgun to my head, and I'm going to blow my brains out."

This began one of the most memorable Sunday afternoons of my life. As this troubled man and I talked, his life story was revealed as one of deadly anger. On the surface, he was successful: a company president who had two master's degrees and a Ph.D. in physics. But his marriage was ending, and the anger he felt was about to end his own life as well.

As I talked to him about his life and how valuable it was, I asked, "Tell me, what made you decide to study physics?"

He responded, "When I got into school, I asked what was the toughest thing to get a doctorate in. People told me physics, so that was it."

I learned that when he was a boy, his mother had frequently told him, "You're so stupid. You'll never do anything in life." So he had responded by imagining a highly intelligent, successful self, which haunted him throughout his life. Now, seeing himself as a failure at marriage drove him to a frenzy of anger that sent him looking for a gun to blow his own head off. He was furious at *himself*.

Fortunately, that gun was never used.

Dealing with Anger

The source of anger is internal, not due to outer circumstances or difficult people. It is due to a basic sinful attitude:

We prefer to listen to shadows and devise a plan for meeting our own needs. We deal with it first by seeking the truth: What does our anger say about us? Most often we concern ourselves with the *object* of our anger, but it reveals far more about us.

Eph. 4:26 says: "Be angry, and yet do not sin; do not let the sun go down on your anger." Anger is valid when its object is injustice toward others or sin. When anger erupts in an effort to protect ourselves, however, it is sin. To put this verse in perspective, we need to look at the preceding verse, which gives us tools for dealing with the wrong uses of anger. Eph. 4:25 says: "Therefore, *laying aside falsehood, speak truth, each one of you, with his neighbor, for we are members of one another*" (italics added).

Several factors help in combating chronic anger:

We must look at the truth.

We are to put aside the false notions that give rise to our anger, the shadows that plague us. Take time to discover what it is within you that triggers emotional outbursts.

We should be accountable to a community of believers who can help us with this difficult issue of life.

". . . for we are members of one another." We need someone who cares for us and will point out the hold that anger has on us, someone who will gently remind us that we are believing a lie. The person who would most naturally fill that role, in fact, might be your marriage partner.

Self-discipline in this area should be regular and systematic.

"Do not let the sun go down on your anger." This is wonderful advice. The habits of rage include thought patterns and ways of acting that have been methodically practiced for years. They will not easily be erased by one or two counseling sessions. You need to substitute new, scriptural ways of thinking about yourself. A daily habit of Bible reading is a good place to start.

Learn to trust that God created you just the way you are. The shadow-self you want to be is not as good for God's purposes as your real self. Find out who that real self is.

Cultivate an attitude of thanksgiving for exactly how God

has made you. Psalm 139:14 says, "I will give thanks to Thee, for I am fearfully and wonderfully made; wonderful are Thy works, and my soul knows it very well." That is the objective: to convince your own soul that His works—including you—are *wonderful*.

What caused Michal to become an angry woman at war? What shadow whispered the lies that drove her to anger? Several factors stand out, providing us with insight. They produced a fertile ground of resentment. We find these same factors repeated in numerous women who experience a lifetime of anger with respect to men.

A dominating father, coupled with an intimidated mother.

Michal's father, King Saul, was a brooding man who could only be described as abusive. His loud tantrums terrorized the palace, and his deep depression was the reason that David and his melodious harp were required in the first place. (See 1 Sam. 16:14–23.) So bitter was his rage that few could even approach him, and his mood swings were the hinge upon which the entire household turned. Saul's opinions were law, which could not be defied or questioned. In those homes where Dad is a tyrant, a little girl spends her life in fear and develops resentment at the prospect of being a woman, a person who, in her eyes, should do anything possible to win over a man.

A wrong value of self.

A father's value judgment on his child, and his general view on the role of women, can have a far-reaching impact. We know that Saul placed little value on Michal. He saw her as chattel and believed he could use her to get even with his young rival, David, by allowing him to marry her. "And Saul thought, 'I will give her to him that she may become a snare to him . . .' " (1 Sam. 18:21a).

I once overheard a father tell his daughter, "The man who gets you is in for a world of hurt." What may appear to be a word of correction, all too often becomes self-fulfilling prophecy.

She touches the "hot stove" in her life.

Given her home of origin, she may see all men through a filter of criticism, a product of her fierce anger toward her father. Most assuredly, she will probe her husband and pore over every detail that might remind her of home. In so doing, she continues to touch the "hot stove" of hurt that she has carried around for years.

As Michal stood on her balcony and watched David dance before the ark, embarrassment was probably only one of her feelings. Certainly, her father had committed many acts that shamed his family—acts of unmanly rage and moodiness.

I believe that part of her hurt was the feeling of being a spectator in the life of her own husband. She watched, but was powerless to influence his thinking, or his actions. Michal felt like an unnecessary fixture in the palace, an outsider in the home she grew up in and a stranger to the position of influence she was born to. She was forerunner to the many women today who feel absolutely unnecessary in their own homes.

For the woman at war, the feeling of neglect is a familiar one, and one she thought she'd never have to put up with again. She saw her mother go through it. She swore it would never happen to her. She thought during her romantic courtship that she had managed to escape the pain she saw in her mother's eyes every time her father ran her down or ignored her. But here it is again—fresh, raw and with her name on it this time. A time bomb is triggered, and it could quietly tick under the surface for years.

When this sensation of neglect surrounds and seeps into the cracks of a woman's spirit, it can produce a number of negative responses. One of the most prevalent is depression.

Neglect can prompt self-doubt. Then a woman may begin asking all the wrong questions: "What's wrong with me?" "Why doesn't he love me anymore?" "Did I do something wrong?" The result is a wrong conclusion: "I'm bad; therefore I deserve to be neglected."

Recently, I sat down with a young couple, Tony and Ann, who are engaged in a growing ministry to people in a number of churches. To help me understand their relationship and how it impacted the work they were attempting with others, I asked Ann, "If you were to die this week, how would your husband's ministry and life be changed?"

A silence fell in the room. With tears in her eyes, she said,

"I really don't think *anything* would change at all."

Tony sat there, wringing his hands, probably wishing he could be somewhere else. He did not need a lecture on the fact that God puts a man and a woman together in ministry to increase their effectiveness. But he did need to occasionally stop his breakneck pace to listen to Ann. He said, "I know I need to communicate to her more that I *need* her, but how do I do that?"

My response was simple. "By really needing her."

In 1 Pet. 3:7, Peter summarizes his encouragement to husbands on the relationship they have with their wives with these words: "You husbands, likewise, live with your wives in an understanding way, as with a weaker [*literally: more delicate*] vessel, since she is a woman; and grant her honor as a fellow heir of the grace of life, so that your prayers may not be hindered." Peter makes it clear that women are equal partners of God's gifts and benefits. So strongly is this idea put forth that even a man's prayer life is dependent on his proper treatment of his wife.

She is "on her own" in her spiritual and emotional life.

Many men shrug their shoulders and exclaim, "Women! Who can figure them out?" Yet 1 Pet. 3:7 says that a husband should "understand" his wife. This starts by simply listening. If a man thinks of his wife's need for attention as an interruption, no amount of gifts or heady compliments will make her feel truly secure. When a man consults his wife and asks for her opinion, he guarantees for her that she owns a special and important place in his heart.

Now it's also true that a woman can send "mixed messages" to her husband. One message can say, "I don't need your support and I don't need you to take responsibility for me." At the same time, she may *want* to say, "Can't you take some interest in my life? Don't you care that we are out of touch as a couple?"

To many a husband, the relationship with his wife and what she wants out of him appears to be a confusing maze. Some men feel that no matter where they turn, they will step on a feminine toe. Therefore, the easiest and least confusing course of action is to simply opt-out of the hassle and to lead their own life, occasionally informing their wives of their whereabouts. Needless to say, this confusion is totally contrary to the design of God.

The patterns of a woman's acted-out anger span a wide range of behavior traits. Each one is designed to be an attention-getting flag and a means of defense. A woman will repeat the patterns she feels most comfortable with and those that have shown the most favorable results from her perspective. Short-term gratification is the goal, with little thought for the long-term harm that results as the pattern of anger erodes the marriage.

The Challenger

Many a woman takes on the role of adversary. She decides to compete with the man in her life. If the only thing he understands is what takes place outside the home, then she'll do better than he is doing and make him feel like a second-class citizen at home.

In doing this, she sets up her own world, independent of him. Sometimes she takes a job, not because she wants it, but just to show him she doesn't need him or his income. The result, at best, is increased distance and estrangement.

Julie was a young women whose anger had driven her to win all her life. She was aggressive, and it was victory at all costs. Her father was an important engineer who always knew and demanded right answers. Early in Julie's life, he had begun to turn Julie into a tennis star. Now, Julie handled everything as a win-lose venture, everything from a game of checkers to a simple conversation. She always had to come out on top, always had to have the last word.

No wonder her marriage to Mark turned into war. Julie explained it to me this way in his presence.

"When I first started dating Mark, I knew I had driven off every boy I'd ever been around. I figured my problem was I just couldn't find a man who was strong enough. Mark seemed so strong that I didn't think I'd have a problem. Sure, I could beat him on the tennis court, but he was good at other things and seemed so self-assured."

"Mark," I asked, "did you know you were getting such a competitor for a wife?"

"Sure," he replied. "I just didn't know she'd never let up. It's like she's got her foot on my neck and just keeps pressing it down. What's with her? Not only that, but she keeps reminding me of every time I've blown it, even in front of my friends."

He gave this example: Three nights before our meeting, Mark and Julie had invited friends over for dinner. Afterward, Julie suggested they play a card game. Throughout the evening, Mark was subjected to constant criticism. Julie opened the game with, "It might be best if Mark and I aren't partners, I hate to second-guess how he'll bid." In recounting the evening, it was clear Mark felt no respect from his wife and believed she saw him as inferior.

I also learned that Julie's *omnicompetent* father was a man whom she viewed as perfect. Her mother, on the other hand, was unpretentious and quiet, constantly depreciating herself in front of family and friends. Julie had told herself, "I'll never be like that. If that's what it means to be a woman, no thanks!" From childhood her quest in life was to be like Dad and to avoid being like Mom.

Sitting in my living room, and in front of Mark, she said, "Maybe it would have been best if I'd never gotten married." I could feel Mark sink deeper into his shoes.

Deep down Julie was still a little girl, afraid of being vulnerable and determined not to allow herself to display any needs. Her view of what it meant to be a woman was dreadfully out of focus.

Fire and Ice: The Two Great Sexual Clubs

Unfortunately, for many an angry woman the sexual relationship is not to be enjoyed but used. It becomes a club that is used to humiliate and frustrate her husband. Instead of being an adventure and a joy that creates unity, it produces anxiety and drives partners away when used with the wrong motives. Some men have performance anxieties, and what may appear to be only a minor "off night" due to fatigue becomes a test of his masculinity.

Books are filled with discussion on the problems of female frigidity. The passionless woman, though, is not what we're focusing on. Instead, I want to examine the supreme objective behind the sex act for the angry woman, which is the need to punish her husband.

First, barring some physical or emotional scar that causes a woman to refuse sexual pleasure, that may be a deeper need to gain control. For some, sex is not the problem at all. If a woman feels out of control in every other area of her marriage, then the sexual relationship may be the one realm in which she is able to assert herself and remind her husband that she too is a factor to be reckoned with. For some women it becomes a call for identity, a cry: "Notice me. I'm a person, too."

The sexual union is the wrong place to negotiate for recognition, however. What couples who go through these types of frustration need is the ability to communicate fully. The sexual relationship is a place where a couple communicates totally. The first place a communication breakdown shows itself is in bed. Things left unspoken by a wife will be in her thought process during sex. These could vary from simple questions—"Is the door locked?" "Did we put out the cat?" "Are the children asleep?" "Did we forget to pay the bills?"—to more complicated and unresolved conflicts such as, "This guy hasn't spoken two nice words to me today" or "I haven't liked his attitude this whole week, and I don't like it now."

Often these thoughts are brewing, but are left unspoken. If a husband senses these things at all, it can come across as an icy distance when he wants his wife to be the most responsive.

She *is* responding, but she's responding to *everything* in her day, not just the short overture she was given while in bed. When a woman makes love, her response encompasses her entire day, perhaps much longer, and her whole frame of reference toward her husband.

If a woman allows her unsettled conflicts to communicate a physical disinterest in her husband, further complications will arise. Men view their sexual prowess as evidence of their youth, virility and desirability. These wrong messages create an atmosphere in which a husband will feel the need to distance himself from his wife because of a growing sense of pain over his inadequacy. He will attribute this injury—or from his viewpoint, disaster—to his own sexual failure, not to the unresolved conflicts his wife may feel. He sees it that way because that is the frame of reference in which he has encountered the problem.

The other beating a wife can inflict upon her husband is to use the "fire" side of the sexual club. In this her tactic is to downplay the satisfaction she gets from their sexual union, communicating her dissatisfaction in the harshest way possible and often at the most humiliating moments. This kind of hostile confrontation is the most heartless cut of all.

Cheri and Larry had been married for four years. Point-blank, and in front of him, she told me, "I'd been very active sexually before I became a Christian. When I met Larry, I thought all that experience would be carried on in marriage."

I watched Larry drop his head slightly and shift his feet under the chair as she went on. "But he's never ready when I'm ready. Aren't *all* men supposed to be ready?" The implication was that Larry was less than a man, an insinuation that was not lost on Larry. I watched him lower his head even more. "When we do manage to have sex, he acts like he can't wait to get it over with—like he's got another appointment or something."

Larry, clearing his throat, responded, "Yeah, she asked me a couple of weeks ago if I was going to a fire—"

"That wasn't two weeks ago," Cheri interrupted. "It was more like a month and a half."

I asked, "What else do you hear, Larry?"

He gave a list of equally damning statements that evidently had been ringing in his ears throughout their short marriage. "I don't say the right things. I'm not aggressive enough. I'm not slow enough."

I had to hold up my hand to Cheri to keep her from interrupting as he went on. "I don't come nearly close to satisfying her. I'm not as good as any of her former boyfriends. And I also get a list of what she used to do. I'm supposed to follow directions and do things the way some old boyfriend did."

Moreover, it was "fair game," in Cheri's view, to mention Larry's "problem" at any time, even in the presence of friends, bringing him to silence and a feeling of total rejection. Sex had become Cheri's ultimate weapon, retaliation for anything from Larry's forgetting a loaf of bread to being late for dinner. Sometimes it was simply a first-strike when she'd had a hard day, and getting even with him was a way to get even in general.

It wasn't that Cheri was totally insensitive. She saw herself as someone who felt deeply about other people. It was just that she carried around this angry chip on her shoulder and felt the need to hold at arms' length any man who tried to come close to her. She refused to give up control in her life and was going to maintain the dominating edge, no matter what the cost. In her case, it was costing her a husband who loved her. Ultimately, it was also making her a very lonely lady.

Ridicule

The ability to strike a verbal blow and draw blood in an argument is a skill that for many angry people has been sharpened to perfection. This ability, like any other, often comes with "practice, practice, practice."

A number of years ago while I was a student, a friend invited me to dinner at his home. At the front door, he issued this warning: "Jim, be careful. You're entering the war zone. It's every man for himself."

What went on after that could never pass for dinner conversation. Cutting remarks flew. The art of character assassination had been sharpened to perfection. I asked my friend on the way back to school, "Does that happen all the time?" He replied, "Every night."

Some people learn to relate to others only on combative terms. The strong survive and the weak—well, they just crawl off to die. The subconscious baggage of our childhood homes moves across the honeymoon threshold along with the bride and groom. Those raised in combat never take off their helmets. They have lived with it so long that they see it as normal. "The family that bounces off the walls together stays together." Now, if those people did stay together, the damage would be minimized—but they marry unsuspecting peace-lovers. They marry people who did not come equipped with a helmet.

Love Coupled With Accountability

As a family, there must be not only a desire to love each other but a commitment to be accountable to do the details of love. Love requires certain "chores." They may seem unpleasant. At times they could even be described as drudgery, but they must be done, nonetheless. No matter how much fun it is to play with the baby, diapers must be changed. That principle holds just as true in adult love. Accountability is one of those "chores" that keeps love growing.

A number of years ago, a pastor friend related this experience. He had been teaching his children about being "accountable" in family relationships. As sometimes happens, he found the tables turned on himself.

They had spent the summer on an island off the coast of Canada, swapping places and pulpits with another pastor. But for my friend and his family, it was more stressful than they could have imagined. One unexpected crisis after another arose. On top of that, a short stay by relatives and in-laws turned into a long stay. My friend had reached the breaking point and a little bit more.

Sitting at the dinner table one evening, he watched his wife discipline one of the children in a way he didn't like. He told her as much. She blew her stack and told him where he could go with his advice. The children burst into tears and ran crying from the table to their rooms.

One by one, my friend visited each room, reassuring each child that the family was safe. There would be no divorce, and he had no intention of going where Mommy said. Last, he visited his youngest daughter, five-year-old Tiffany.

She crawled on his lap and said, "Daddy, why don't you go and tell Mommy you're sorry?"

He replied honestly, "Honey, I will. I know I should. But, Daddy's heart is hard, and I don't feel like I can just now."

Tiffany looked at him in a knowing manner and answered, "Then I'll pray to Jesus that He will soften your heart."

She then placed her hand on his head and prayed. "Dear Jesus, please make my daddy's heart soft again and help him to love Mommy. Amen."

She then looked up and gave him a simple assignment in accountability. She said, "Daddy, I'm going to tell you what you should do. You go to Mommy and tell her you love her; then she'll tell you she loves you. You kiss Mommy; then she'll kiss you. Then you come right back here to me and tell me what you've done. OK?"

Tiffany had a handle on how to work out the problem of anger in the best way possible. She got to the truth about her "client's" problem. She was part of a committed group that was going to help work things out. And she asked him to start a procedure that she could hold him accountable for. The laughter that punctuated her mom and dad's apology became part of a beautiful memory that would never be forgotten.

Sweetheart, always remember . . . the man is the head of the house, but the woman is the neck. And it's the neck that turns the head.

> —*Advice given by a mother on her daughter's wedding day.*

11

Bathsheba, the Manipulating Woman

The issue of control and who has it is pivotal, affecting each marriage partner's sense of worth and security. As we have seen, when a husband abandons any pretext of leadership, he loses even the illusion of respect, and with it goes his masculine role as protector and provider. Feeling much less a man when he goes home than when he is at work or play, he simply chooses not to go home. When he is forced to be at home, it is much less painful for him to stay uncommunicative and aloof. He stands off from the torment of facing his lack of influence. He now sees himself as only slightly necessary.

On the other hand, some wives believe themselves completely unable to have a voice in their own lives. Having what they see to be only limited options, many respond with bitter and silent submission, others with open warfare. Yet a significant number of others choose to manipulate, developing a "skill" I call *emotional remote control*. They give up the closeness with their husbands that God intended and find a distance and lack of respect for their spouses and ultimately for themselves.

I believe that Bathsheba was a prime example of this type

of woman, and that we can learn a lot by examining her manipulations.

David and Bathsheba

First, it's interesting to note that the watershed decisions of David's reign were made as a result of Bathsheba's "influence." Consider:

- David's sin of lust and adultery (2 Sam. 11:1–4).
- The murder of Bathsheba's husband (2 Sam. 11:5–24).
- David and Bathsheba's son Solomon is named his successor after David makes a promise to Bathsheba (1 Kings 1:11–31).

It's also interesting to note that in none of these events does Bathsheba bear any blame for David's wrongdoing. Many people are highly sympathetic toward her position. They argue that when faced with a man who was the sole law and appeal of the land, she no doubt was powerless to stop his advances. Yet adultery is a two-way street. It involves encouragement and consent. A woman's sexual influence over a man is a great power for oneness or for humiliation. The sense of leverage it gives to some women can and often does become destructive.

Such was the case of a woman I'll call Dorothy.

Anatomy of an Affair

Dorothy was a mother of three and in her early forties. She had been raised in a home nestled in the Bible Belt of urban Alabama. She met her husband, Brian, at church, and after sixteen years as a full-time housewife and part-time babysitter, she returned to a career as a computer programmer.

Sitting down at a conference, she tugged at my sleeve. She sadly batted her eyelashes as she looked into my eyes and said, "I've always been a terrible flirt. Somehow, I never saw it as anything but harmless fun. You know, a way to get boys to notice me. Now I'm in big trouble; can you help?"

A slender, pretty woman, Dorothy explained that she had allowed three pregnancies and poor habits to cause her to gain fifty pounds. "I felt like a frump," she said. "When I looked in the mirror, I just couldn't see anything feminine."

She went on to explain that Brian was "a very steady and faithful sort of guy." Rarely did Dorothy ever hear a complaint from him about her weight. The problem was, she also never heard a compliment. "Jim, he never says, 'You look nice. That's a great looking dress. Thanks for the beautiful dinner.' When I try to pry compliments out of him, I wind up feeling crummy. You know, like it wasn't his idea in the first place."

For years, Dorothy had brooded over the lack of excitement and romance in her life. She had grown accustomed, in her childhood and teen years, to being that sweet, blue-eyed "belle of the ball," a feeling she had not experienced since the end of their honeymoon. "I didn't know what to do to get him to notice me."

Three years before, she had lost her fifty unwanted pounds. She had joined an aerobics group, and for over two years had been lecturing other women on the benefits of weight loss. Yet, in her own home and in the romantic relationship with her husband, she had seen none of the benefits for herself. "I'll wear a nice bathing suit or a flimsy nightgown, and all I get is a raised eyebrow and what might be a longer look than usual from Brian, but nothing else. When I ask, 'How do I look?' I get the same tired old answer, 'Great.' I'm so tired of just looking great." Dorothy had slowly become a powder keg of discontent.

Recently, she had gone back to work at a small marketing firm to fill up the time on her hands. Omar's small but growing office seemed like a safe place to restart her career. Omar was in his late forties, bald and short. But he had a quality that Dorothy never expected to encounter when she took the job: He noticed her. And she began resharpening her dormant skills of flirting.

At first it seemed like such a harmless game. What could be hurt by turning a few heads at the office? What was the harm in looking into his eyes just a little longer than usual? After all, he knew she was a married woman and what church she attended. She shared her "personal testimony." Omar had begun to introduce her as his ace employee and "pet Christian." Frequently, he would call her into his office to praise her work, and not a day went by without him referring to the way she looked. In front of customers or salesmen, Omar would say, "Sweetheart, you just light this place up every time you walk through the door."

Going to work became the one thing she looked forward to, not because of the pay, but because she felt more feminine there—more desirable, more alive.

Now, she confided, "Two months ago, when it was my birthday, we had a little celebration. After everyone had left, Omar gave me a kiss. Just a *little* kiss—and a hug. He held me a little too long. He said, 'Happy birthday, sweetheart,' and gave me an envelope with a hundred dollars in it. 'This is a birthday bonus,' he said. 'You don't have to tell Brian about it, just use it for a little mad money. And let's keep it between the two of us, OK?' As I drove home, all I could think of was that look in Omar's eyes and the kiss and hug that I had allowed. There was something about the danger that frightened me, but something about it made me feel sixteen again."

I asked Dorothy, "Has there been any further physical contact between you and Omar?" She sighed, "Yes there has. Nothing sexual, just holding and kissing. I know that if I walk into his office and sit on the couch, he'll get up and come to me and it will begin. Every time I drive to work I tell myself not to do that. I know what will happen. I don't want to lose my marriage. I don't want to displease the Lord. I sit at my desk and just grip my computer. But eventually I give in and walk into Omar's office and sit down. I don't know why I do it. It's like taking some kind of romantic drug. I know it will kill me, but I just have to have it."

Brian's Response

As I listened to her story unravel, my first question to Dorothy was, "Have you told Brian anything about what's happening at work?" Her answer surprised me. "Yes, after Omar started coming on to me, I told Brian that my boss was starting to flirt and that I was kinda liking it. I told him that I had probably started it myself by being a little playful and humorous, so it wasn't all Omar's fault. Of course, I haven't said anything to him after the kissing began." Her eyes filled with tears. "Brian just looked at me and told me he hoped this didn't mean I'd have to quit—that we needed the money. I was so mad and so hurt I could have hit him."

The ability to manipulate a man's attention by sexual attraction is an electricity that gives some women, like Dorothy, the power and dominance they seek. It usually begins in childhood by being "cute" in front of Dad, batting her eyes and doing little things that get his attention and applause. When the opposite sex becomes a new interest, intensity is redirected toward gaining social approval and the admiration of female friends over her "special abilities" in attracting boys. After marriage, it is only natural that her charms are aimed at her husband. However, if he is unresponsive or lacks enthusiasm, she may not feel the same power as in the past. Essentially she remains "wired" for it, nonetheless. Womanhood can simply become a power trip, and femininity something to be used.

Besides sexual manipulation, "punishment" is another strategy used by many women to manipulate. This punishment is meted out in a number of ways:

Shame.

Most women have discovered that a man's greatest weakness is in the area of his ego. To rise above the man in her life and expose his lack of thinking, his financial weaknesses, his childlike habits or some insecurity will visit her vengeance on him in a way little else could. This little routine is displayed at the most embarrassing moments: in the couple's Sunday school class, at social gatherings, when the boss comes to dinner, and in a most devastating manner in the bedroom. It can become the ultimate weapon used in marital conflict, the court of last resort. In wielding this weapon, she becomes something of a cross between "the dragon lady" and a reminiscence of her husband's mother. While both of these characterizations are repugnant, they do offer one "redeeming" result to a woman who is not getting the attention of her husband—*power!*

Flirtatiousness.

Even in Christian social circles it occurs. I have listened to more than one husband complain during counseling that his wife is a flirt. When it is done out of his sight, as he suspects it is, she becomes a prime candidate for an affair. When it is done in front of him, it serves as an insult, designed to get his attention or the attention of another man. In either case, it is a public slap to his masculinity.

Proverbs contains a graphic picture of this type of behavior when it says: "As a ring of gold in a swine's snout, so is a beautiful woman who lacks discretion" (Prov. 11:22). The beauty and desirability of such a woman is lost. In her overwhelming need for attention, she has only displayed a soul that needs immediate help.

Withholding love.

Some women have grown up with parents who disciplined by use of the "cold shoulder." It seems natural for them to employ that same means to communicate to their husbands that they are in disfavor. To a husband, it becomes a game of twenty questions to see if he can guess what he's done wrong now. For most men it is so frustrating that it only serves to drive them further away.

When it comes to withholding sex, most women have a rationale that is impeccable. One woman quietly but firmly said, "If he forgets to call me when he's going to be fifteen minutes late for dinner, I'm just not in the mood for lovemaking. Maybe if I'm not in the mood enough times, then he'll get the point and start being more thoughtful."

Several issues surface in the face of this reasoning. What this woman is communicating subliminally is that she does not actually enjoy the sexual relationship with her husband. It is only a tool, to be used in getting her way or as a reward if he has been "good."

Dr. Dan Kiley writes about the use of sex as a manipulation and the damage it does to the one attempting the manipulation:

> The woman's hollow view of herself as a sexual creature is confirmed; her ability to enjoy sex is decreased;

her restlessness and longing are increased, as is her anger; and her bitterness toward life is focused on her man and, in some cases, on men in general, locking her into a pessimistic view of love.[1]

This tack will only continue to drive a wedge between her and her husband. Sex has far more to do with how husbands and wives embrace each other's souls than it does with how they touch each other's bodies. Sex is a gift that God has given to marriage partners to promote oneness. "And they shall become one flesh" (Gen. 2:24). God's instructions on the subject are clear:

> Let the husband fulfill his duty to his wife, and likewise also the wife to her husband. The wife does not have authority over her own body, but the husband does; and likewise also the husband does not have authority over his own body, but the wife does. *Stop depriving one another*, except by agreement for a time that you may devote yourselves to prayer, and come together again lest Satan tempt you because of your lack of self-control. (1 Cor. 7:3–5, italics added)

A third form of manipulation used by women is a "false vulnerability." "Men melt with tears," one wife told me. This was how she got her husband's attention. "I know that if I can just get myself worked up enough to cry, that's all I need to get his attention. He's a pussy cat inside and doesn't know it."

I asked her, "How about you? How do you know what *you* are inside? How can you tell real pain from the phony stuff?" She had no answer.

Communication that is deceptive and is intended to take advantage of someone else only serves to make the person who uses it increasingly out of touch with his or her true feelings. It can also backfire should the husband become aware of what is being done to him. The little boy who cries wolf—or the little lady—eventually comes to the same end.

"Martyrdom" is a fourth means of manipulation. The "righteous victim" becomes an ongoing role designed to illicit sympathy. Pity can rarely be equated with love, yet there are

---

[1]Dr. Dan Kiley, *The Wendy Dilemma* (New York: Avon Books, 1985), 128.

women who outfit themselves for that unattractive role. And it is usually accompanied by a genuine sense of unworthiness and inferiority. Unfortunately, it leads not to a husband's genuine attention and affection but to his further withdrawal. It develops in an entire family the sense that "something's wrong with Mom."

The "martyr mom" has a crippling effect on her daughters, unfortunately. Joan of Arc may play well in the history books, but girls from those homes often grow up with a warped and distorted idea of what it means to be feminine.

During a singles conference in Colorado, I was approached by a bright and attractive young woman who, at first glance, seemed like she was not long for singles conferences. As we talked about her future I asked, "What about marriage?"

"Well, I just don't know," she said. "When I get close to a guy, I just freak out. In fact, I wind up trying to find out something wrong with him just so we can break up."

As we discussed her background it became apparent that she had come from a home with a mother who played the role of martyr. For my young friend, independence from a man had become her goal in life. She was willing to do anything to avoid becoming like Mom.

The fifth common ploy used in manipulation is "guilt." Guilt is practiced in some homes to perfection. With an icy stare, a silence, or cold words, the offending husband is put in his place. One man expressed it this way, "When she gives me that look, I feel like I am being brought to heel. I hate it. I shouldn't have gotten a marriage license. I should have gotten a dog license."

The results of the treatment in the minds of both partners is counter-productive. For many men, thoughts of their own mothers and the type of discipline and lectures they received as a child flash back to mind. And while they may have loved Mom, they did not want to marry her. Guilt, like so many of the other emotionally manipulative tools, is a negative reinforcer. Research shows that while guilt-conditioning may produce behavioral change, it causes resentment and anger.

A sixth manipulative tool is "competition." Because a man's world is outside of his home, some women choose to get his attention by competing with him and beating him at a career. If she cannot get his attention with cooking, her looks, or her needs, she resolves that he will pay notice to her paycheck. For some women, work is fulfilling and enjoyable, but for the manipulator the job is also another weapon to be used in the ultimate battle at home.

Children, too, can be used in the manipulation game. Appalling as it may seem, an unhappy woman can see her child as being someone who needs her when her husband does not. The child looks at her with love, clings to her and provides the cuddling that she is starved for. Many expectant mothers have told themselves, "Maybe this baby will hold our marriage together." That simply does not happen. Good marriages are designed to hold children together; children are not created to hold their parents together.

A husband also notices his wife's preoccupation with her child while she excludes him from her affection. Some of these men, admittedly a small minority, know that their wives are busily searching for tenderness. The vast majority of men—those who have found that contentment comes with keeping a distance from what they see as a demanding woman—only feel relief from their wife's constant need for companionship.

A woman who has misplaced her center of self-worth, placing it on the backs of her children, tends to be a "smothering mother." Many a disappointed woman with a firstborn son has worked hard to make him "the kind of man I wish I had married."

For a disappointed mother who has a little girl, the child can become too much of an extension of herself. All of the hurts and pains that the mother has endured can be projected onto her daughter. Mother can, by proxy, live out her own life through her daughter. She must protect and coddle her darling at all cost. She has to make sure her little girl never has the pain she herself has experienced, because in a very real sense the little girl is an appendage of the mother, one she is nurturing and protecting. This type of behavior is not always easily observed, but shows itself in ongoing anxieties that interject a mother into her daughter's life time and again.

How Does a Wife Create Change Without Manipulation?

In each of the above strategies of manipulation, change is only short-term. The only fundamental and lasting effect is that of further distance between husband and wife. A wife's habit of putting her husband through a series of marital management techniques communicates very clearly that she has little or no respect for him.

For the wife who uses these tools, the nagging questions remain: "How important am I to my husband in reality? Can he love me just for me, or does he show me his attention only when I pry it out of him with my guerilla warfare tactics?"

What, then, are the most effective ways a woman can break into a man's world and get his affirmation, attention and action without resorting to inappropriate influence?

The Right "Tactics"

She starts by turning her back on manipulation.

The first thing for a wife to do when she sees herself in a cycle of manipulation is to *honestly admit the problem to her husband and ask for his forgiveness and help.* This will immediately communicate a new respect for him. Just the process of squarely addressing the subject may provide the kind of hope for a newness in the relationship that an ignored woman hungers for.

Even if a wife must carry on a one-sided attempt to energize her marriage, there is still great hope. The Apostle Peter recognized the prospects of a one-sided attempt at marriage. He writes to women who may not only be wed to an unbeliever but to a man who is actively disobeying God:

> In the same way, you wives, be submissive to your own husbands so that even if any of them are disobedient to the word, they may be won without a word by the behavior of their wives, as they observe your chaste and respectful behavior. (1 Pet. 3:1–2)

She makes a commitment to minister to him, not manage him.

Marriage is an opportunity for the believer to minister. We have an outlook, however, that tells us life is supposed to be wrapped around our own happiness.

A good marriage, though, is a lifetime calling to a ministry. The goal of that personal ministry is to make a significant difference in the life of one other person.

I am sad to say that I have seen spiritually mature and extremely gifted women who have had magnificent ministries to others while they have marriages and mates that they have given up on and only refer to in an embarrassed and apologetic manner. I've talked with their husbands, who silently remain in the background and have beat a hasty and intimidated retreat from the spiritual leadership of their home and even their own lives. The disrespect these men have felt and the impotence to approach their wives with their own ideas have taken a fearful toll on their own outlook on life. As a group, these "spiritual drones" are among the angriest men I know.

The wife who has impatiently dealt with her husband and concluded "It's no use, I'll just pray for the guy and get on with my ministry" will find a tremendous lack of fulfillment, even in the midst of success. There must be a renewed vision to view that man as the major part of her ministry. Her first calling from God is to be his "helper" (Gen. 2:18).

The woman who truly sees herself as a servant of Christ should ask herself hard questions: *I may be committed to this marriage—but am I equally dedicated to the man that is in the marriage with me?*" Often, a woman feels a glow of dedication on the subject of *marriage*, but when faced with her *partner*, her outlook becomes sour and pained. *"What are my husband's greatest needs and how can God use me to supply them?"* Every one of us have two sets of needs: those we want to have met and those we'd rather ignore. Many women start their ministry with their husbands by hammering away at the needs that the husband would prefer to ignore. But like any other ministry, we should start by first meeting *felt needs* in a way that will be appreciated. The final question, and the one that will give credibility to the others, is this: *"In what ways do I need to grow and develop in order to minister more effectively?"* People who minister to others should apply the standards they are setting for themselves first. As God supplies our shortcomings, our confidence grows that He can use us to meet our mate's needs.

She affirms his right choices.

There are large numbers of men and women who have simply given up on relating to and pleasing their spouses. They feel that they can't do anything right, so why bother. There are, in fact, many other positive tools that reinforce the right and constructive behaviors in a marriage. I often hear from women about their need for compliments, and rightly so. But it escapes some women that their husbands have a need for compliments too.

The wife should set a "trap" for her husband, catching him in the act of doing something right; then make a big deal of it, being sure she tells him why she appreciates what he is doing.

A wife can give her husband a great boost by simply thanking him for doing tasks around the house, and for taking time to listen to her when she's going through a rough time.

Little statements like that, which show a genuine appreciation, make an impact on even the most hardened man. For some women, it may mean swallowing some pride, but those statements will ring in his ears the entire day.

She appeals to his values.

Deliberate, prayerful and daily effort should be given to affirmation. But when that shows a decided lack of response, as it will with some men, a careful appeal to his values and what a wife knows her husband is already committed to can bring about change. There should be a sit-down, face-to-face talk, carefully spelling out expectations, coupled with a wife's expressed confidence that he will change because she believes in him and appreciates what he ultimately stands for.

By doing that, a woman can clearly spell out what she needs and why. More importantly, she has appealed to her husband's values and what she knows he stands for already. She has not delivered him a final ultimatum, but an adult-to-adult request. Men respond much better to a straightforward, simply-laid-out statement of fact that puts that ball in their court. Keep in mind that this should be followed up with favorable verbal strokes for the positive action he decides to take.

Loving Confrontation

There is a world of difference between an uncontrolled emotional outburst and a loving confrontation. In the first instance the person is "out of control" and has declared "war" just to vent frustration and anger. When the person finishes he may feel better, but most likely he still will be face-to-face with a problem that refuses to go away. This type of problem-solving does not have a solution in mind, just a desire to get even or, to "put someone in his place."

Solomon, a man of considerable experience with women, shows us in Prov. 21:19 a typical male response to life with a contentious woman: "It is better to live in a desert land, than with a contentious and vexing woman." That is precisely what men do in response to a contentious woman, they remove themselves to places of isolation. The objective of confrontation should not be a change of behavior only. That is too short-sighted. The goal must be a renewed understanding, closeness and communication that will move the relationship toward greater cooperation and love.

A second variety of marital strife takes the form of low-level warfare—known as nagging. Nagging is confrontation that is subtle but frequent. It carries with it a notion that nothing will ever change. The tone of a person who nags is that of hopelessness: "I know you won't do this, but I'll remind you one more time." Of course, the one more time quickly becomes one hundred more times. But the husband does not change. In his mind, change represents a surrender to this type of verbal torture, which he thinks would only encourage more abuse. Therefore, he remains perpetually committed to non-action.

There are better ways for a wife to confront.

She must defuse any personal anger she carries into the confrontation.

She must begin by taking careful stock of the kind of "self-talk" that is being spoken and believed. If she is constantly murmuring, "That guy will never change," or "He just doesn't care a thing about me and my needs," or "What's wrong with me that I can *never* get any cooperation out of him," then she will walk into confrontation filled with rage, and will face a no-win situation. "For the anger of man does not achieve the righteousness of God" (James 1:20).

She must discern the legitimate needs that both she and her husband have.

She must ask herself: "What does my spouse want from me or from our marriage? Can I supply them in part, or in whole? Am I willing to supply those needs first, if he will be willing to listen to my own needs?" The ability to approach other people with their needs in mind is disarming. It is also the mark of someone committed to loving other people. More importantly, it gains a hearing in any situation and quickly becomes the hallmark of a successful person. A top motivational speaker points out, "You can get anything in life you want by helping enough other people get what they want."

The buck must stop somewhere. The wife must clearly lay out what she needs and the way it would help her and the marriage. Along with that, she should spell out the alternatives and what the results will be if things continue to drift along as they are.

She can formulate her own statements, like:

> "Sweetheart, am I creating a problem for you by asking you to use the clothes hamper? Is there something that I am communicating or some way that it makes you feel? When you don't, you make more work for me and communicate to me that you just do not care. From now on, what does not go into the hamper does not get washed. I refuse to let it upset me. So I'll just keep loving you without washing your clothes."

She must manage a crisis, not a husband.

On occasion, there is the need for a full-blown crisis. The line must be drawn and the spouse must know that things will simply not be allowed to continue as they have been.

Let's return to the situation with Dorothy, who was on the verge of an affair, and finish out her story.

When Dorothy quit her job and went to her pastor to seek help in managing her situation, it was because she had little or no hope of help from her husband. You'll recall she had approached Brian before the relationship became serious and had received no help. Instead, she felt taken for granted and used. She was fearful of what Brian's reaction to the truth would be. What she needed was a point of no return where she was committed to action and Brian was committed to listen to her emotional needs. She finally insisted they get counsel from their pastor, and he provided the kind of accountability for both of them that set their marriage on the road to recovery.

Many women view the remedies I've suggested beneath their dignity. "After all," they say, "if the guy really loves me, he'll do this routinely, won't he? If he doesn't, then it must mean there is something wrong with him, right?" While this type of rationale has a ring of truth to it, it is a take-it-or-leave-it mentality, destined to produce radical bumps in any marriage. It also shows an underlying belief system that disputes the notion that marriage is a ministry. A wife does not have to center her life around her husband's every desire and whim, but she does have to creatively dedicate herself to minister to her husband, working toward the ultimate objective of Christlikeness within the bonds of matrimony.

An intent of Peter's statement concerning a wife's submission—even to a husband who is an unbeliever—is this very idea of Christlikeness. When he says, "In the same way, you wives . . ." he is referring to what he has just written about the lifestyle of Jesus. Without a doubt, it is one of the most difficult passages to apply in all of Scripture:

> For you have been called for this purpose, since Christ also suffered for you, leaving you an example for you to follow in His steps, who committed no sin, nor was any deceit found in His mouth; and while being reviled, He did not revile in return; while suffering, He uttered no threats; but kept entrusting himself to Him who judges righteously. (1 Pet. 2:21–23)

Time after time, God shows us that if we are willing to trust Him and do things His way and in His time, the reward is far more satisfying than our temporary, and partial gains.

If you want a word well said, ask a man. If you want a job well done, ask a woman.

—Margaret Thatcher

12

The Woman at Work

You could always count on Alice. She was energetic, efficient, and never known to complain. Why wouldn't the church want to call on her to spearhead the fund-raising drive for the new Christian education building?

As the nominating committee's discussion drifted on, one member raised an issue: "But Alice has a husband, three kids and she works. Besides, she's already heading up our Sunday school department."

The committee chairman trotted out the age old advice on delegation. "If you want to get the job done, find somebody who's busy." The group nodded its collective approval. "Besides," he continued, "if Alice can't do it, she can always say no."

Unfortunately for many women like Alice, their compulsiveness and their need to be needed will not *allow* them to say no.

Alice's husband, John, was understandably proud of his wife's seeming limitless capacity. However, his own feeling about his role in her life was that he was merely an appreciative bystander. A favorite phrase of John's was, "Whatever makes her happy, that's what I want her to do." Since they'd been married for eighteen years, most people who knew them thought that whatever it was they had, it must be working.

171

The reality of their life, however, was far different from the efficient facade that was portrayed in public. Alice and John were two of the loneliest people in the church. They could easily have been classified as "married singles." Officially they were married, but their lifestyle and their schedule kept them apart. They shared few activities and even fewer real interests. I gathered from talking with John that if Alice didn't plan Sunday dinners where she invited people over, he might not have seen her at all. But he was quick to add, "Oh, I'm not complaining. I'm just glad to see her busy and happy."

As I got to know this couple I learned that they had steamrolled their lives into aimless activity—*anything* to avoid communication. In fact, each had come to depend on the other's inability to confront problems. For Alice, work was not something she did to feel fulfilled or even to earn extra income. It was a place to go to avoid pain.

Busyness can often become a narcotic painkiller that serves to deaden the pain of an empty life. While people like Alice are *not* in the majority among working women, many do go through the same thought processes. A large number suffer from the guilt, loss of communication, and stress that plagued Alice. Today's working woman is in the majority. In 1997, nearly 60 percent of all married couples in America were dual earners.

Choices and Tensions

The expectations placed upon women continue to accelerate alarmingly. For a woman to discover where her responsibility and its accompanying pressure ends is like peeling the layers of an onion. The new doors open to women have become a blessing and, at the same time, a curse.

Generally speaking, women find themselves pulled emotionally in a direction opposite that of men. The result is increased tension between men and women.

I am frequently asked by single women, for instance, "Why are men so afraid of commitment?" The answer lies in understanding a man's nature and how he views the world. When a man passes his late twenties and moves deeper into the career-building stage of life, his world lies outside the doors of his home. To maximize his impact "out there," he often feels that he needs to simplify the maintenance of what happens in the private, "nonproductive" part of his life. A marriage and a family limit his time and how he uses it. The increased "responsibility overhead" causes some men to see life narrowing, chaining them to obligations they do not feel ready for. Indeed, some men will never be ready for too much responsibility. If they have to go home, they can't go out with the boys. If they have to buy a dishwasher and a station wagon, they will not be able to get that new sports car they've been eyeing.

It will surprise, and possibly irritate some women to learn how most men view a woman's choice to marry—for they see it as a choice that brings a whole set of new opportunities. She can, if she chooses, accept the traditional role of full-time wife and housekeeper. This role, presumably, allows her time to devote herself to creative home economics and ministry within the church (provided her husband's income is sufficient to supply both of their expectations). Moreover, no one will raise an eyebrow if a woman chooses to stay home, especially in Christian circles. On the other hand, a woman can choose to move on in her career and maximize her own marketplace potential. Most people feel this is a growing financial necessity, but for some it is simply a matter of enhancing their lifestyle or seeking fulfillment. Regardless of her choice, the majority of men believe that marriage opens doors of opportunity for women.

Many women today, however, feel as if all of life's alternatives are demanding exploration—all at once. They feel they have somehow "fallen behind," that they are unable to satisfy everyone. For the Christian woman, identity cannot be based on the latest trends in *Cosmo* or *Woman's Day* but on God's Word. The Bible is the standard that transcends culture and time. The Scriptures are specific enough to give us a broad direction, yet the instructions are not so limiting that there is not room for individuality or calling. In Titus 2:3–6, Paul tells more mature women that part of their ministry is to "*train* the younger women to love their husbands and children. . . ." The idea is to coach a woman in the process she is already involved with, that is, the God-given bent to nurture a family with love. There is no reprimand to stay within the four walls of the church and home. There is no indication in Scripture that women are not endowed with the same sorts of gifts as men, though there are directions as to her priorities. Even these are generally in line with the way God designed women.

A common cry today is that Christianity is too limiting or irrelevant for modern women. That is not so. Even in her own household a woman is to be anything but a passive observer who merely sits about and waits for direction from her husband. Paul says, "I counsel younger widows to marry, to have children, *to manage their homes*, and to give the enemy no opportunity for slander" (1 Tim. 5:14, NIV). This passage, among others, points out that women are to be involved in supervising the home. This is not intended to create a two-headed monster with conflicting claims to household leadership, but rather a system of shared confidence, prayerful guidance and mutual support. Stephen Clark, in his extensive work on the roles of men and women, writes:

> The husband's headship over the house neither relieves the wife of responsibility nor makes her passive. Nor does it make her a simple servant in the house. Instead, the wife's subordination to the husband expresses an order of authority with the wife's ruling function carried out subordinate to the husband's.[1]

More often than not, a woman's worst accuser is her own conscience.

Some women feel they are caving in under the pressure of too much to do and not enough time to do it well, too many expectations from too many people and not enough emotional support and understanding from the people who know them best. Where does a woman look for direction in the way she plans and schedules her life? Where does she go to be nurtured herself?

A woman would like to feel she can go to her husband for guidance. Unfortunately, this is a position he may have abandoned. He may have done so because he does not feel needed,

---

[1]Stephen B. Clark, *Man and Woman in Christ* (Ann Arbor, Mich.: Servant Books, 1980), 57.

or because, compared to his omni-competent wife, he feels intimidated. Until the last forty years or so, this kind of thinking was unheard of among men. In the Judeo-Christian heritage, husbands assumed management of the house and development of the people within it. A man's guidance was to be sought and his view respected. The television sit-coms many of us grew up with don't play well in a culture that is trying to elevate women to a world of perpetual responsibility. *Father Knows Best* seems far too sexist a title for today, but it simulated the kind of stable atmosphere wherein each family member felt secure and loved and where the father held a constructive, pivotal position.

The biblical role of a man does not end at the doorstep. Many men feel they are good providers because of their ability to make a living. But too often the very people they live with are squeezed out of their priorities. In God's economy, it is this priority that displays the trustworthiness and reliability of any man. Paul gave Timothy a list of qualifications for any man who would be an "overseer" in the church:

> He must be one who manages his own household well, keeping his children under control with all dignity (but if a man does not know how to manage his own household, how will he take care of the church of God?). (1 Tim. 3:4–5)

The role of manager applies to every Christian man. His job is not finished when he comes home. As far as God is concerned, men are to put the management of their homes high on the list of priorities. Home is the site of every man's ministry.

Even if a man is fulfilling his obligations at home, however, there is still far too much pressure on women today, with their many-faceted roles. For one thing, consider the conflicts of the Christian woman who may find herself "in command" at work, and struggling to be "in submission" at home. Not only that, the working woman usually finds herself bearing an unequal share of work required at home. No matter what the checkbook says about her contribution to the family income, the home is still looked upon as a feminine burden. Over the course of a decade, *USA Today* surveyed more than 100,000 people in over 100 public opinion polls. The results were startling. They write:

> Consider this: In this age of liberation and equal opportunity, 94 percent of all women who live with a man say they do more work around the home. And the men agree. Surprisingly, however, only about 1 in 5 women—21 percent—wish the men would do more around the house. This is the key to understanding the conflict for women. . . . *As they expand their horizons, they are not all sure they want to give up the thing that has always given them self-esteem—the ability to take care of their home and family.*[2]

Can She Really "Have it all"?

Women have been led to believe that they can "have it all." A successful career, a happy husband, well-adjusted children, a "meaningful" ministry in the church, a trim figure, a gourmet kitchen and a clean bathroom all await the woman who is organized and energetic. Solomon advises us in Eccles. 9:10: "Whatever your hand finds to do, do it with all your might." In Solomon's day what your hand could find to do was a relatively narrow assortment. In our supersonic, hi-tech society, we have little time to do things with all of our might. Yet women have a far greater inclination to try.

As a result of pressures at home and at work—not to mention her husband's retreat from leadership—a woman is likely to feel she is beleaguered by enemies on all sides.

What is the most common enemy stalking the private world of today's women?

Private Enemy Number 1: Stress

Stress has become a major factor in the workplace. Companies hold seminars, and psychological gurus are paid large retainers to deal with the problem. For women who work, stress can become a critical predicament because women tend

---

[2]Anthony M. Cassle, *USA Today*, "Tracking Tomorrow's Trends" (Kansas City, Mo.: Mcmeel & Parker, 1986), 51. Used by permission.

to internalize their problems more. To further complicate matters, most of the solutions these company lectures focus on are male-oriented. Ideas like taking up a hobby or joining a health club may sound fine to the average male, but to the working mother with children and a husband waiting for dinner, they offer little or no help.

The woman at work also subjects herself to a set of inner attitudes that create pressure. It is as if a tape is being played over and over, and as she believes its message about her, the pressure cooker of too-much-to-do-and-not-enough-time-to-do-it can heat up past boiling. Here are some of the attitudes that create or intensify stress.

Tape #1: "I must perform well at all cost." There is a bumper sticker that reads, "The best man for the job . . . is a woman." Many firms have found that to be the case. Women seem to be tireless workers. Many assembly plants both here and abroad have noticed that women pay greater attention to the detail required for assembly work. There are fewer errors, less injuries on the job, and greater productivity. A plant manager told me, "The women here have a passion to do the job right."

Of course, the desire to do a job right is not a negative attribute. But a woman may refuse to lay down a task because it has not been done to her satisfaction, or because she is afraid she will be judged more harshly because she is a woman. This can and often does lead her into fatigue and a belief that she never does *anything* well. You know you are listening to this "tape" when:

- the day ends in disappointment with a sense of frustration and nonaccomplishment;
- absolutely everything must be done to its highest standard;
- criticism or even a question becomes a crushing blow;
- the words "I'm sorry" seem to begin every sentence.

Tape #2: "Everything around here depends on me." Some households come equipped with their own self-installed martyr. "I don't know how this family could make it without me" is the battlecry of this home. She refuses help in the kitchen and spends a great deal of time organizing the closets and drawers of each member of her family. She does not understand that it is much easier to organize the people once than organize the drawers a hundred times. Besides, if that happened someone might see her sitting down, and she needs to be seen working.

Tape #3: "I have a score to be settled." A woman can enter the working arena with an insatiable desire to balance the scales of her life. If her sense of self-worth was hurt by what she sees as simply a lack of finances, then more money can reimburse her for that former pain.

If it is a matter of doing something that other people notice ("After all," she reasons, "who notices a housewife?"), then an important busy job may provide that.

In the case of Alice, the overworked Sunday school director, she felt she had something to prove. She told me, "My father wanted a boy. I guess I've always thought that I had to do more and be better just to stay even."

Tape #4: "Why don't people love me as they should?" This type of damaging thought comes from the belief that love is something to be earned. Often, a person who feels unloved will have the notion that if she does more, she will be loved more. When the affection she seeks is not forthcoming, she reasons, "I'm not doing enough."

This type of thinking begins a tedious cycle of task-oriented behavior that is self-defeating. A person who operates on this level will do so both in and out of marriage. All friendship becomes a matter of barter and exchange, and rewards from the job must be given exactly on the basis of the work involved. If it does not happen, then the person blames himself or herself. After all, "Something must be wrong with me."

The values that produce this thinking are ultimately rooted in our concept of God. Our view of who He is and how He establishes and maintains a relationship with us is the foundation of our security as a person. If the One with the highest standards of all, the Creator God, accepts us and loves us apart from our performance, why must we raise our standards in gaining approval with people?

Larry Crabb writes:

> My need for security demands that I be unconditionally loved, accepted and cared for, now and forever.

God has seen me at my worst and still loves me to the point of giving His life for me. That kind of love I can never lose. I am completely acceptable to Him regardless of my behavior. I am under no pressure to earn to keep His love. My acceptability to God depends only on Jesus' acceptability to God and on the fact that Jesus' death was counted as full payment for my sins.[3]

Performance-free love is available only to the believer. Other people patch together strategies to gain from relationships the type of approval God gives out freely. But these tattered devices all break down in the course of normal living. For many, marriage is the first place where the material begins to wear thin. The plans of many people center on their abilities to gain the attention and approval of others by doing what is traditional, well-thought-of. The result is an outer shell of a behavior pattern that is, in essence, painfully empty.

Tape #5: "Why are these things happening to me?" Many times people go through great stress because they have been conditioned to believe that, at least for the Christian, life should be trouble free. They know things happen to others, but somehow they've formed the opinion that they, by virtue of their faith, have an excused absence from pain. Jesus made a special point to communicate, in the Sermon on the Mount, that "the rain falls on the just and the unjust" (Matt. 5:45). But when the first raindrop hits the life of a woman who is listening to this tape, she assumes that something is wrong with her. The natural conclusion is that bad things are happening because somehow she is not living up to her full calling as a woman.

Tape #6: "I am just no good." The need to hide is a great stress producer. Many people see their lives as a failure and feel the pressure to hide from everyone. A question that haunts most of us is, "What would all these people say if they knew who I really am?"

Women who work fight the feeling of failure at least sporadically. They have so many things to do and tend to try to do each one in a way that would please—please their employ-

---

[3]Larry Crabb, *Effective Biblical Counseling* (Grand Rapids: Zondervan, 1977), 70.

ers, their fellow employees, their families, or their husbands. With that many goals, failure is going to be a fact of life. But it does not mean that the woman who "fails" in any one duty is inadequate, nor is "failure" a brand to be carried on the working mother's conscience.

An unsettled conscience adds more stress to an already busy day. The insecurity produces estrangement from God and from the people who give us the most support.

Tape #7: "I give up." The final step in a habit pattern of stress is to disconnect the alarm. It comes from a sense of helplessness born out of frustration. It is not a surrender of our inabilities to God's grace; it is a surrender *period*.

How Do I Get Out of Here?

The good news is that the stresses of the working woman can be overcome. They need not be a source of gnawing tension that eats away at your relationships at home.

The following are some steps to help you escape the stress-trap.

What is it I am saying to myself?

The place to begin reducing stress is to start listening to self-talk in a conscious manner. What is being said? Are those things to be believed? What makes them sound believable?

Things that are brought into the light of day seldom stand the test. The tendency is to hide our fears from others so well that, in the process, they remain hidden from ourselves as well.

Ask yourself a question like, "The last time I felt angry or depressed or nervous, what created that problem?" In the very act of describing, the stress-producing self-talk "tape" will become audible. Then you will know what untruths you are dealing with and how to best face them.

What is the truth about myself and about God?

Someone can become so accustomed to the false messages about his or her life, that the truth does become "stranger than fiction." After discovering the self-talk "tape" that is clearly untrue, the next step is to determine what *is* the truth.

The clearest truth is going to be found in the Scripture, and that is where your focus must center. Phil. 4:8 states:

> Finally, brethren, whatever is true, whatever is honorable, whatever is right, whatever is pure, whatever is lovely, whatever is of good repute, if there is any excellence and if anything worthy of praise, let your mind dwell on these things.

Obviously, God's opinion of us and the value He places on our well-being is infinitely more significant than that of our boss, or husband, or children, or that fellow who honked at us at the stoplight. Unfortunately, our world far too frequently shrinks to the size of the last person who criticized us.

Instead of remembering that God esteemed us as important enough to die for, we fix our minds only on the person who thought little of us. In fact, our relationship with God is meant to dominate every area of our thinking, all of the time.

Confess the lies that are ruling your mind.

The only means we have of maintaining fellowship with God is the claim we have on the blood of Christ and the assurance we are given in the confession and forgiveness of our sins (1 John 1:9). That process means agreeing with God about the basic wrongness of what is being practiced in our lives. It is the next step in the beneficial process of taping over wrong thinking and stress-producing self-talk. Identify what is "malpractice of thought" from the objective standards of Scripture, and begin to dwell on the assurance offered by the Father God who deeply loves you.

The goal, in the end, is to replace wrong patterns of thinking—which govern your feelings and actions—with God's right patterns of thinking. (See Rom. 12:1–2.)

Now What Do I *Do*?

The mind is not the only front on which the battle against stress must be waged. You must be willing to make *real* changes. Some ideas may seem obvious, but here are a few you should consider:

1. *Have fun.*

Life is a gift from God. A healthy step in recovering from stress is learning to recognize and capitalize on the quotient of fun that God has given to each of us. Pleasant circumstances are not what we live for—but neither are they something to be avoided. There is nothing inherently spiritual in a monastic mind-set. Paul sets a wonderful balance for us in how to deal with providential circumstances in 1 Tim. 6:17:

> Instruct those who are rich in this present world not to be conceited or to fix their hope on the uncertainty of riches, but on God, *who richly supplies us with all things to enjoy.* (Italics added.)

We do not serve a God who is opposed to fun. And most people take themselves much to seriously.

Learn to have fun again.

2. *Have self-control.*

People who are under pressure sense that life is out of control. They feel pulled along by the strongest current running through their life at the moment and are fearful that if they stop paddling madly, they will end up who knows where. When they begin to take responsibility for things they can control—even if it's only what they eat, or what they do with the first fifteen minutes of their day—the pressure will begin to diminish.

Self-control is one of the signs that God's Spirit controls your life (Gal. 5:22–23).

Self-control should start in small, easy-to-digest portions. It is easy to get ambitious too quickly and discouraged even quicker. If a diet is too ambitious, try a diet once a week or a lunch-only diet. To have self-control is to turn to our compulsions or problems one at a time and say, "No, I won't do *that*, I will do *this* instead."

3. *Have dreams and goals that are worthy of a child of God.*

We don't have to give up our dreams to grow up. Even though we live in an age where the rich and famous have become "heroes," there are values that transcend finances and power. Burn-out comes quickly when we have lost direction but continue to race the engine. As Solomon said, "He who loves money will not be satisfied with money, nor he who loves abundance with its income" (Eccles. 5:10).

For many women "lost" in the child-rearing years and feeling saddled with the need to work, there no longer remains an objective that is bigger than they are, that involves the power of God and that they can plan and pray for. But how does one go about establishing worthy goals?

A good place to begin is to take a completely new perspective on your life. Try looking at your life from the *end*. Ask the question, "What must I see at the end of my life to know that I have accomplished what God intended for me to do?

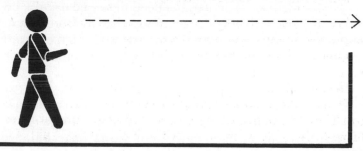

Most often, those things that seem desperately vital for us at age twenty-two, pale to insignificance at age seventy-five. Maturity tends to clarify our values. Working for that new car may seem important, but when we view it with the perspective of a lifetime, few of us would trade away more time with our children to get it. Yet without thoughtful and prayerful planning, that is exactly what we do.

While we must give some time and effort to providing material things, if they make up the sum total of our life's work, then life will be pointless indeed. The Christian who struggles inwardly with this sense of pointlessness is a prime candidate for stress.

In studying Scripture, I can find only two things of eternal value in which we can invest our time: people and the Word of God. (See Acts 24:15 and Matt. 24:35.) If our goals reflect these values and our time is spent wisely in these areas, then our dreams will have a true and satisfying purpose.

4. *Practice saying no.*

When we have spent time prayerfully developing proper goals, we become much better prepared to say no to plans and desires that don't live up to our dreams. They may be worthwhile—but not necessarily for us. Often, it is not that we have no plans, it is that we cannot bring ourselves to tell someone no. An invitation to take on a responsibility does not mean it is the best thing for us, or that someone else could not do the job better.

The need to be needed is the enemy that we too often allow to creep into our schedule. Learn to defeat this enemy and you will reduce a fair amount of stress in your life.

For women in particular, the need to say no usually begins at home. Especially if you are employed away from home, you will need to overcome the guilt that tries to latch on to you as you begin to say no to your family when it comes to certain stress-producing factors.

For instance, it is perfectly all right to tell your twelve-year-old that he is old enough to make his own sandwich for lunch, do his own laundry, pick up his room. It is perfectly all right to ask your husband to take out the garbage, balance the checkbook (or help you do it), drive the kids to baseball practice, or to spend some time listening to problems weighing on your heart. It is all right not to be the slave of your husband and kids, *particularly* if you work outside the home. In fact, it will help train everyone in responsibility, love for one another and giving if you *don't* shoulder all the burdens like some kind of neurotic martyr mother. If you keep on filling in all the gaps, denying all your own needs, what are you really saying to your children and husband about life? That it makes no demands? That someone will always come along and pick up after you?

Being the household "slave" *plus* working to supplement the family income will wear out anyone, no matter how energetic. It won't do to listen to the little tape in the back of your head that says, "If you were better [stronger, smarter], you could manage to do all that's demanded of you." Not only should you erase the tape, you should begin to spread the responsibilities around. You'll be surprised and delighted by how much stress this one change alone will relieve you from.

Trusting a friend or spouse to help in dealing with the

pressures of work and the unspecified but endless demands at home is absolutely essential. Building new habits and seeing a reduction of stress will happen only through recording and reporting daily successes. It may be measuring the times that you have said no. It might involve recounting the sound of negative "self-talk tapes," or how you decided to take control of your life in some small way. But most certainly, it will mean taking someone into your confidence and asking for help.

Two are better than one because they have a good return for their labor. For if either of them falls, the one will lift up his companion. But woe to the one who falls when there is not another to lift him up. (Eccles. 4:9–10)

In the event of cabin depressurization, an oxygen mask will drop down. Should you be traveling with a small child, place the mask on yourself first, then on the child.

—Commercial aviation preflight
instructions to passengers.

13

Stopping the Cycle in Your Children

If the struggle for control in marriage could be confined, kept between the husband and wife, that would be one thing. But marriages have a way of producing children, and children catch the fallout when war erupts between Mom and Dad. The problems and the pain of men and women quickly become the problems and the pain of their sons and daughters.

Parents do not plan to deliberately endow their children with unresolved pain, but we know it happens. The conflicts and longings of youth then become a part of parent-child relationship when that child is grown. Deut. 5:9 aptly summarizes this cycle when it assures us that the iniquities of the fathers will be visited on the children "to the third and fourth generations." This is a simply statement of fact: We do reproduce after our own kind; we give to our children what is deeply ingrained within ourselves.

The problems addressed in this book—wounds that stem from distant or weak men married to dominant, abused or over-protective women—are the problems almost certain to develop in a child, ensuring his or her need for long-term emotional help and constant encouragement. Paul Meier, in discussing the research for his book on child-rearing, states:

A definite majority of the neurotic children I have treated come from homes in which there is a *weak, passive father and a domineering, smothering, overprotective mother.* Also in preparation for this book, I have sat for many days in the library of Duke University Medical School poring over research findings on parent-child relationships—what types of parents produce what types of children. The research literature describes hundreds of syndromes, and in a majority of them there is a weak, passive father and a domineering, smothering, overprotective mother.[1]

In short, unresolved hurts, a sense of abandonment and lack of affection are long-lasting emotional bruises. And no matter how many times we told ourselves as a child, "I'll never treat my kids this way," invariably we continue the cycle. Studies have shown that alcoholics and child abusers produce alcoholics and child abusers. Tragically, we do pass along the hurts we've been dealt.

For the Christian, there is another dimension to consider also. God. When Jesus called God "Father," He meant it as a word picture, designed to conjure up warm and close thoughts toward God. It was intended to spark our own thinking about the fellowship we are to have with God. But for many people, the picture that flashes to their mind when they think of their "heavenly Father" is that of someone who is preoccupied, aloof and cold. Sadly, it is usually an accurate reflection of the only father figure that person has ever known.

To be a parent is to be the foundational influence in the lives of your children. If parents decide to opt out, or to minimize their effect on their children's lives, other designers— money, peers, video games and television—stand waiting in the wings to do just that. It is too easy to step back and simply allow a child to swirl about in the current that society and technology provides.

Recently, I heard a story about a mother who went into a suburban shopping mall in Houston, Texas, where she buttonholed a shopping clerk in a toy store. The woman said she

---

[1]Paul D. Meier, *Christian Child-Rearing and Personality Development* (Grand Rapids, Mich.: Baker Book House, 1977), 17.

wanted "a toy that will keep my child entertained all evening. It must be educational," she went on, "but I want to be sure that when he's playing with it, he will be totally involved and I won't have to come running to him every fifteen minutes." After a lengthy search of the store and dozens of rejected ideas, the aggravated sales clerk said, "Ma'am, what you're *really* looking for is a parent, and we don't sell those."

The point I'm underscoring is this: We parents have a tremendous influence over our children—and not only over *them*, but over their marriages, their children, and perhaps even *their* grandchildren. This influence can be for health or harm.

How can we build our sons into strong and sensitive leaders in their own homes? How can we train our daughters to have confidence in relationships without the need to dominate or manipulate? How do we raise children who are healthy, whole adults, and so stop the cycle of tension and covert warfare in marriage?

Let's take a look at the answers to these questions, first, in relation to our sons.

Raising Sons Who Are Active, Not Passive

There are very definite building blocks, a foundation that you can lay today to raise your son to be a strong and sensitive leader tomorrow. Yes, you can prepare him even as a boy to become a mature, stable, and caring father and husband later. These building blocks are not difficult to put in place, but they do require commitment and consistency on your part.

Build his confidence. The cornerstone of confidence is committed, unshakable love. When a child experiences love and learns to give it within the family, that child is on his way to becoming a healthy adult. It is not a *self*-confident "bravado" that builds a boy into a good husband. It is a confidence that comes from knowing, "I am loved here in this home and will always be loved by these people. I can give myself to them even when it hurts." The family is the best place to cultivate unconditional love.

The other side of the confidence coin is a dedication to the truth. Love without truth is nothing more than empty sentimentality. It may feel warm and comfortable, but even children know that this kind of love will never stand the test of time and exposure to the elements of real living. To take a child and excuse his improper behavior in the name of love is to send him off into a world he is unprepared to face. It condemns him to a fairy-tale standard of reality. Truth makes love meaningful. To expose a child to "love" without truth makes him deceptive; to expose him to "truth" without love makes him cutting and critical. A mixture of both will give him the gentle confidence he will need to become a healthy man.

Intercepting a boy from becoming a passive and disinterested husband and father will involve the practice of discipline, superimposed over a feather bed of unconditional love and acceptance. Love opens the heart-door for discipline to have its greatest effect. Dr. Ross Campbell writes in his book *How to Really Love Your Child*:

> We can be confident that a child is correctly disciplined only if our primary relationship with him is one of unconditional love. Without a basis of unconditional love, it is not possible to understand a child, his behavior, or to know how to deal with misbehavior.[2]

Love provides the basis for the responsible qualities that are necessary in the development of a man who cares and leads.

Because it is in the nature of all males to strive for respect—which is confidence with his peers—careful foundations must be laid to support a man's self-image as provider, standard-bearer and the driving force in his family. The more a boy feels that he can depend on his family and the significant people in his life, the less chance there is that he will turn to wrong means of confidence-building—namely, the acquisition of things and the self-promotion of empty achievements.

Give Him Time, Not Just Money

Many parents give their children money or expensive toys, but not their time. Committing time to a child says

[2]Dr. Ross Campbell, *How to Really Love Your Child* (Wheaton, Ill.: Victor Books, 1981), 29.

"you are important"; committing undivided attention says "what you think and feel is important." The act of looking into a child's eyes and listening to him is the greatest gift a parent can give.

A child learns what is truly significant by observing what is important to Mom and Dad. If all day and every day we spend our spare time polishing the car, a child naturally assumes that "the car and how it looks is of utmost importance." What we watch, what we read, the things that capture our attention and even the moods our world invokes do not go unnoticed by even the youngest of children. They are experts on what really makes Mom and Dad tick.

Children do not overlook our attitude toward money and the "high" that it produces when it is the center of their parents' lives. Money, or the sense of what it can give us, has become a very dangerous shortcut to emotional security. Advertisements tell us that the key to lasting satisfaction is found in a certain product. A false sense of values and the pseudo-security that money brings will form emotional distance in little boys. If the parents' lifestyle says good feelings, friendship, and nurturing relationships come when you have the right amount of money, then is it any wonder these little boys grow up to be men who continue to trade the care and nurture of a family for ways to get and use *more* money?

Who is there to teach children that a caring family must be built, not bought? Mom and Dad. Time spent with our children in a caring and thoughtful manner communicates that people, conversation, and caring for someone else give true satisfaction. Today, we so frequently throw about the notion of "quality time." If we cannot spend hours with the children, then "quality" minutes will do the trick. So after days and weeks of inattention and nonconversation, we bundle the family of strangers together and force a little fun on people who seldom talk and find they do not even know each other.

One father who found himself in this habit pattern related this little nugget from his family's last trip to the zoo. After forcing the kids to turn off Saturday cartoons, they found themselves speeding down the freeway on their way to fun. One of the children leaned across the back of his car seat and asked, "Dad, is this quality time today?" In a child's world there is no "quality" time; there is only *time*.

Challenge Him—Don't Allow Lazy Thinking or Living

A young person needs to learn that ownership and responsibility go hand in hand. The more things we have, the more our time is spent maintaining what we have chosen to accumulate. Instead of promoting maturity, though, we often allow children to enjoy the ownership and use of things but assume the responsibility for them ourselves.

When I walk into a home where young children live, and watch the mother scramble about to pick up the toys, I am tempted to ask, "Are those your toys?" Instead of calm instruction and daily discipline, we too often communicate fantasy living and crisis management. This is precisely the thinking that a husband who had decided to be an escapist has cultivated throughout his life. While the problems might have been easy to correct at age five, they are tougher to break than rawhide at age forty-five.

These parental influences, as I have said, are especially important in the rearing of boys. Other influences, of course, are vital in raising both sons *and* daughters who are healthy and whole.

Dealing With the Common Habit of Blame-Shifting

The ability to duck responsibility is a skill begun in childhood and perfected as an adult: A problem is always closely followed by the knee-jerk reaction of blame-shifting. This results when a child is allowed to be irresponsible. Every problem is someone else's problem.

Escaping blame has been practiced as a science since the Garden of Eden. It is part of the sin nature. I have spent what seems like a lifetime driving long and short distances with three small children in the backseat and can testify to the wide streak of blame-shifting that runs through the character of every individual. No pinch, push, shove, or ill-spoken word is ever an original offense. Every evil seems to be provoked by someone else.

The problem with blame-shifting is that, over time, it solidifies like concrete.

Jeffrey was a graduate student who stayed in our home for a summer. His maturity contrasted to his likable qualities. He was twenty-six years old going on fourteen, a little boy in a big body. His mother had always picked up after him, and we distastefully found ourselves doing the same thing—while listening to his excuses and even making up a few of our own.

After a visit he had made to his home, I talked to his mother on the phone to find out when he would arrive back at our place. I learned that he had asked her to call me at the last minute from his hometown airport in the expectation that I would pick him up when he arrived back here in California. After explaining that I had other plans I asked, "Does he do this often?"

She replied, "Oh, yes. I guess he just expects other adults to treat him like his own parents do." Then she added an interesting commentary. "He's a good boy—a messy boy—but a good boy."

Those are sad words to hear about a fourteen-year-old, but to hear them concerning a twenty-six-year-old graduate student is tragic.

The list of excuses from Jeffrey and others like him are endless. ("I had to rush to class, so I had no time to get my clothes out of the washer." "Sorry I ate the pie last night. You didn't tell me it was for company.") This continual rationalization comes from growing up in a foam-rubber environment. When little boys are allowed to escape softly from failure time and time again, they become big boys who point to other people's failure but have never learned to recognize it in themselves.

Help Them Develop Their Own Values

Nothing is more truly our own than an idea that is the product of our own thinking, or objects and activities for which we choose to take responsibility.

Many children, however, are accustomed to having all their opinions formed by the pressure of the powerful people in their lives—including smothering mothers, domineering fathers, and alluring peer groups. In the end, the children do not know what they truly believe and their values shift, depending on whoever is exerting the most influence over them at the time. They continue to remain, in their own minds, "little people," whose duty is to avoid conflict and pain. In marriage, they gravitate toward the role of the weak husband or the wife who suppresses bitterness while she allows herself to be abused.

When a child is placed on the witness stand in a courtroom, one of the first questions asked about his competence to testify is this: "Do you know the difference between right and wrong?" It is surprising how many children cannot answer that question clearly. They have been taught that "what's right feels good and what's wrong feels bad." This is because the duty parents have in building values all too often does not center on the absolute standards of right and wrong. They gravitate toward what is convenient, inexpensive, or that which brings recognition.

We tell children "do not touch . . ."; "do not say . . ."; "do not do . . ." But we often forget to tell them why. Providing reason and teaching a lesson for future reference takes time, thinking, and effort. And the dividends include character- and value-formation, because they grow internally into a child's thinking.

When I was a youngster, my mother and father would caution me on proper behavior when I was to be a guest at someone's home. "James, you're not to take candy or gum unless someone offers it to you." The words which followed that type of statement were even more important: "You are a gentleman, and a gentleman always waits patiently for things to be offered." I could walk into the house not only armed with a list of do's and don'ts but with a picture of *who I was to be* printed on the inside of me and the knowledge of how that was to influence my behavior.

Well-honed values are, quite properly, the products of home and family. To reach the character of a person requires the time to understand and a commitment to long-term results that the family environment is best suited for. As wonderful as Christian education is, it will never replace the direct life-on-life impact of a family.

Work at Being Close—Learn Good Communication

Children are greatly affected when parents talk down to them, or fail to understand how to communicate with them. Their parents' inexperience puts the children at a disadvantage, and they assume that the lack of understanding is their fault, not their parents'. *Telling* is not *teaching*, yet some parents give instructions and then assume the child should know what to do.

Good teaching requires time with a child and requires that a parent disclose himself and what he thinks to his children.

Recently, I was engaged in conversation at church with a visitor from China. Our family seldom, if ever, is among the first out of the parking lot, and on this particular Sunday my children were increasingly impatient with how long it was taking to get home to lunch and an afternoon of fun. After the third or fourth interruption of my conversation, I made a mental note to teach a lesson on manners when we got home.

Shortly before lunch, class was in session on the living room couch. "You know, kids," I began, "we don't just go to church to hear a sermon, sing songs, and attend Sunday school. Why *else* do we go to church?"

After much discussion, the subject was exposed: "Dad, we also go to church to love people and to help them know and love Jesus."

I picked up on this readily. "You know, that is exactly what I was trying to do for that visitor today when you were interrupting us. And he was being made to feel as if he were a bother. Would you like to be lonely, in a foreign country, and feel that no one had time to talk to you?"

The children sat there, sober as three judges. Two of the three judges had tears beginning to form.

"Dad, we didn't know what you were talking about."

"Yeah, Dad. Nobody ever told us!"

To which I replied, "I know. It's my job to teach you these

things, and I respect you three and think you're old enough to learn this lesson."

Later, at lunch, a little prayer went up that "we'd get to know our friend from China."

Work to Build Connectedness Between Siblings and the Extended Family

Isolation only breeds lonely, independent, self-centered people. (Precisely the characteristics in husbands that drive women crazy!)

The rugged individualist is the hero in our culture, not the person who cooperates and learns to help others. Technology is also allowing children to grow up isolated and unchallenged by the need to cooperate. My childhood was filled with imagination, and the collective efforts of other boys and girls used to create make-believe worlds of armies, knights on horseback, Indian attacks, and little houses on the prairie. Too often, a child's world today is built around a video screen and interactive toys that try to substitute for real people. Families have become smaller, and the isolated world of many children has shrunk to the size of the space in front of the television. While children hunger for the stimulation of other people, you know they are being fed on a steady diet of money and things.

A number of years ago when our children ranged in age from three to seven, I came home to a household brimming with bunny rabbits. Each child in the bunch had made a set of rabbit ears out of paper and neatly taped a ball of tissue on his rear for a tail. Each one sported a set of handmade whiskers and was holding a carrot in his "paws" as he hopped through the living room. There among them, to my amazement, was the eight-year-old resident cynic of the neighborhood. Andrew, the only son of two working engineers, regularly showed up at our door with his latest expensive toy, but always found it difficult to play with other children.

My wife took me aside. "They wanted me to help them become bunnies. When Andrew came, he looked at them and said, 'That's dumb.' But after watching for a while, he wanted to be a rabbit, too. So there he is!" I had never seen our little "nay-sayer" more happy. The unstructured and wide-open world of a child's imaginative play cannot be improved upon.

Emphasize Play More Than Competition

Children need to cultivate the ability to work and play with others. Competition at an early age has replaced unstructured play in many suburbs. Conflict and the hurry of growing up in the fast lane causes many children to succumb to the crippling effects of stress long before they are emotionally equipped to handle it.

Having coached high school football, I saw youngsters who, at the age of fifteen, already had seven years of uniformed football experience under their belts. Instead of it being an adventure, instead of it being enough just to play the game, football had become for them a place where they had to prove themselves and exhibit an air of professionalism far beyond their childish level of maturity.

Children who are subjected to the adult world of "life and death" competition are placed too soon in a climate of stress, where rules are absolute and the language and intensity can hardly seem as "child's play." It is also a world in which little boys cannot afford to be vulnerable or cry. This hard shell of "macho-ism" fits a boy like socks on a rooster. But he will continue to try to wear it if that is what the authority figures in his life demand.

When a child learns to relate to others in a child's world of make-up words, relative rules, and fantasy endings, he associates with his peers on his own level and becomes a much more "connected" and socially developed person. But when life is force-fed to him at an accelerated rate and failure takes on a new and fatalistic impact on his developing personality, he seeks only to hide from others, and may try to escape in increasingly harmful ways.

Children who have been short-circuited into adulthood and tossed to the competitive winds of society without a parachute are candidates for major dysfunctions in later life. Little boys believe they must become a candidate for a Rhodes Scholarship or an all-star quarterback, and little girls play the part of vamps before they know what love means. Given those alternatives, children are predetermined to feel a failure at something, sometime. If there is no room for failure in their world and the sense of competition is too great, the outlook they carry around for their own tender lives becomes warped and grim indeed. Eventually these pressurized youngsters become prime candidates for marriages in which each boy sees himself as someone who should never fail in the world and each little girl grows up feeling that she should have and do it all.

Children in upper-middle-class America can easily be isolated by affluence and fed stress by a silver spoon. The expectations placed upon them by their parents mount with each benefit they are given. The collection of things, money, and benefits becomes an enormous burden that they no longer feel they are able to bear. Because they are only children, yet find their lives in the fast lane, they see their lives as "out of control." When they are detached from close, heart-to-heart relationships with other children and see themselves embroiled in competitive relationships, disaster results. David Elkind, a professor of child study at Tufts University, writes:

> Adolescents are very audience conscious. Failure is a public event, and the adolescent senses the audience's disapproval. It is the sense that "everyone knows" that is so painful and that can lead to attempted or successful suicides in adolescents who are otherwise so disposed. Hurrying our children has, I believe, contributed to the extraordinary rise in suicide rates among young people over the past decade.[3]

Some degree of self-evaluation in children is healthy, if it is used properly. But our society is taking children who are thirsty for play, and giving them a drink out of a fire hose. If parents are not observing the stress level in their children and if they are out of touch with how the children are feeling, then the competition that is forced upon them can become nothing more than adults looking for their own self-esteem through

---

[3]David Elkind, *The Hurried Child* (Redding, Mass.: Addison Wesley Pub., 1981), 20.

the efforts of a child who happens to share their last name.

Comparison has always been and always will be a human problem, and it is a problem for children as well. Paul warns against it in 2 Cor. 10:12:

> For we are not bold to class or compare ourselves with some of those who commend themselves; but when they measure themselves by themselves, and compare themselves with themselves, they are without understanding.

No one wins in the subjective game of human comparison; either we come out ahead and become proud, or we fall short and become insecure. It is a "heads you win, tails I lose" proposition, filled with self-doubt. But competition leaves little room for doubt, one wins and one loses. And if a child is consistently on the short end of the stick and lives in a nonsupportive home that fails to express unconditional love, the emotional overhead of stressful competition is not worth whatever benefit can be gained by it.

None of these factors in and of themselves will take a boy and predispose him to becoming a passive or distant husband. But if they are present and the foundation of love is incomplete or confused, then a life that is predicated on escape from pain and unfamiliar with the nature of care in the home will be a natural result. In our society where all these factors are pressing in on us and the divorce rate and phenomenon of single parent homes is on the increase, detached males and disappointed females may become an unfortunate normality.

Dealing With Conflicts at Home

The most important thing a man can do for his children is to love their mother. On the other hand, a woman nurtures her children best and makes them feel secure by respecting her husband. Any solution to the improper development of children must of necessity begin with the relationship of the father and mother. When a child looks at Dad and Mom, the conclusion is inevitably drawn: "That's what I am going to be." That thought can either frighten or comfort the parents.

Too many women have written off their husbands as being

beyond help. The pain of their lives has been too great and the disappointments have mounted one after the other. To the woman who has turned her back on her own future and written off her marriage, this chapter on children may seem like the only hope, a way to start fresh and produce something beautiful and tender. I would like nothing better than to satisfy those longings without the pain of confronting the root of the problem, but I cannot. A woman cannot solve the problems in her own marriage by focusing on her children; she must work first, second, and third on the life she shares with her husband. And then, together, they can help the children.

Building Good Memories

What we do springs from what we remember. In our mind's eye we clearly see how to solve our problems, and whether we want to or not, we draw from the rich memories of childhood. Some adults bring up a bucket from the memory well that is empty and others draw one that is refreshing. As parents, we need to establish goals for what we want our children to remember. In doing so, we should keep in mind that our children will remember us not only for the things we plan but also for our unplanned reactions—the temper flare-ups, discouragements, brooding, distance, and so forth. All of these form the background for the memories of our children. The bright, hopeful side to all this is that our children *will* remember that we had problems—but primarily they will recall how we worked on solving them.

The place to start problem-solving is on our knees. Prayer is often overlooked by everyone except God. In Scripture, however, it is presented as a healthy and necessary component to Christian marriage. First Pet. 3:7 tells husbands to understand their wives and to treat them with honor. The objective of that instruction, according to Peter, is "that your prayers may not be hindered." The prayer life of parents is a treasure in childhood memories.

I asked a very successful pastor what he remembered most about his father, a man who had worked as a construction foreman. "What I remember most," he said, "was passing by my parents' bedroom on my way to deliver papers and over-hearing my dad praying for me. Whenever I get in a jam or I'm unsure of what to do, those words of my dad's prayer ring in my ears: 'Lord, please guide my son and help him to be a man of God.' I'll never forget that."

Children are also fascinated by their parents' romance. When my dad met my mother, he drove a city bus. I cannot recall the number of times they told the story of how Mother was going to the football game with another boy. Dad was driving the bus that night, and he deliberately passed up their bus stop and made them walk. Mother says, "The boy I was with said, 'I guess he just didn't see us.' But I knew it was your father driving that bus." My father never replies—he just sits back, smiles, and winks.

Knowing about his parents' romantic life gives a child a strong sense of security. It tells him where he fits in the world, and that he came into it as a product of love and planning, not by accident.

A woman I've known for years tells about the conversation she had with her children, describing their father's proposal of marriage. Her four children peppered her with question after question about the evening—where they went, what she wore, what they did, and every imaginable detail.

One of the girls asked, "When Daddy finally asked you to marry him, how did you feel?" My friend replied, "Well, I kind of had a flutter in my stomach and didn't know what to say at first."

Upon hearing that the youngest daughter, age six, replied, "Mom, when you felt that weird feeling in your tummy, it was all of us kids pounding in there, saying, 'Say yes, Mommy, say yes.' "

Technology has also produced some wonderful memory-building devices. Old family photo albums may seem boring to visitors, but they are the hit of the household on a rainy day. On rare occasions when our children gather with their far-flung cousins, we also make a special point to borrow or rent a video camera. Regardless of the latest Disney cartoon on the market, family videos are always the most popular choice around the Walker house. The children want to see them, time after time. That's the family they belong to and those are the memories they shared together. Dull or not, it's they who are in those pictures, and that's exciting! There are few "things" a family really needs to invest in, but memories are one of them.

Start and Maintain Family Traditions

A tradition is part of culture, and each family has its own cultural heritage. They are not to be avoided. They are to be cultivated and protected. In our home, Christmas would not be Christmas without a log burning on the hearth and some Christmas Eve fish stew. We also have Bible reading and a story time where one special family story of a long-ago Christmas is told and retold. Birthdays around the Walker dinner table always include each person telling what he or she thinks is special about the person being honored and what he likes about that person. The celebrity of the day sits quietly, listens and glows. These habits and others form for us what makes our family unique and special.

Communicate Family Values and Goals

In many Jewish households, religious celebrations are marked with a father and mother teaching and reteaching what the family believes. It is traditional for one of the children to ask, "Father, why is this night different from any other night?" To which the father replies with phrases that are repeated every year and which he has been coached and schooled by his own parents to recall.

I am sure there are times when these well-worn words seem dull and burdensome and other occasions where they are warm and memorable. But the end result is the same: a continuity in what they think and believe. The process is also vital *communication*. The ability to discuss, explain who we are, what we believe and why has become a missing art form in today's family.

Deut. 6:4–9 contains the most powerful and frequently used directives for the teaching of values in the home. It starts with a view of God: "Hear O Israel! The Lord is our God, the

Lord is one" (v. 4). This statement models the first and most important function of the home in the teaching of values. "Who is God?" Deut. 6:5 tells us, "And you shall love the Lord your God with all your heart, with all your soul, and with all your might." Home is where the theological rubber of our life meets the road. How we react to God and what we say about our belief in God is wide open for our children to see. When we discuss our faith, our children rightly want to know what that means. The answer to that basic question is taught on a daily basis by what we do when no one is looking, what we spend our money on, and how we react or respond to the daily events of life. Like it or not, each parent teaches a course at home on the subject of practical theology.

Following closely on the heels of what we say we believe is the visceral effect our faith should have on our thinking and feeling. Very seldom do children see their parents cry and even more rarely do they see them cry over the hurts and passions of others. But if we as parents want our children to develop a feeling about the principles that govern our lives, it is necessary that they see that those same ethics move us. God and His Word must go deeper than what we say. He must dictate how we feel. "And these words, which I am commanding you today, shall be on your heart" (v. 6).

Recently, I heard a father explaining how his family became involved with the plight of the homeless in America. They had been watching a news program that featured cold and hungry people in their city. Shortly after the program had ended, their twelve-year-old son came downstairs with blankets in his hand and went into the kitchen to make sandwiches.

The father asked, "What are you doing, son?"

The son said, "Dad, I can't just go to bed and think about those men on our streets all cold and with nothing to eat. Would you drive me downtown and help me give this stuff out?"

The father explained that he just couldn't bring himself to say the first thing that came to his mind, which was, "Do you know how much those blankets cost? Do you know how long it will take to drive down there?" He just quietly got on his jacket, picked up some blankets and headed for the door.

It is the unconscious, everyday slice-of-life that teaches our children what we truly believe and why. Deut. 6:7 points to those occasions, saying, "And you shall teach [My words] diligently to your sons and shall talk of them when you sit in your house and when you walk by the way and when you lie down and when you rise up." In short, we parents are to be "on" all of the time.

In closing, I recommend that each family take the time to sit down together and discuss the following questions:

- Kids, what do you think this family stands for and really believes?
- What can I do in order to do a better job of teaching you those things?
- If you could change anything about this family, what would it be?

The answers to those simple questions could not only form the nucleus for family prayer and planning but would be the start of quite an education. They might also be the beginning of a spiritual family heritage. And the impact of that will be the building of strong, healthy, whole men and women for generations to come.

Discussion Questions

Chapter 1
Dancing in the Dark

1. After creating Adam, God saw it necessary to "make a helper suitable for him." How do *you* define the term "helper"?

2. Modern society tells us to be independent and self-sufficient. But God's blueprint for marriage is a coupling of two distinct sexualities. The male body is designed for what roles? The female body is designed for what roles?

3. What is the problem with using your spouse or the world as a mirror of your own performance and self-worth?

4. Do aspects of your marriage make you feel like you're strangers dancing in the dark?

Chapter 2
Who's in Charge Here?
—The Battle for Control

1. Leadership does not mean domination. What did Jesus say and do to illustrate this?

2. What are some common danger signals of a controlling man?

3. When a man's position in marriage is challenged or thwarted, what often happens?

4. If five plus five equals ten in a marriage that involves contact and collaboration between two complete people, how does your marriage add up?

Chapter 3
What Makes Men Tick
—and Women Tock?

1. How do most men build their self-esteem? How do
   women?

2. Name some differences in how men and women communicate.

3. In what ways do men and women approach romance and
   sex differently?

4. What steps can you take to begin entering your spouse's
   "world"?

Chapter 4
The Building Blocks of Passive Resistance

1. For both men and women, the seeds of negative thinking and resultant habits are planted in childhood. Describe how conflicts at home, a hostile worldview, and inadequate or missing role models for men contribute to this problem. What promise is found in 2 Corinthians 10:4–5?

2. Name some examples of wrong values that cloud a man's thinking.

3. Why are male friendships important for husbands? Should a wife be her husband's best friend?

4. Reflect on your childhood. What building blocks were laid during that time of your life?

Chapter 5
The Withdrawn Man

1. When does passive-aggressive behavior often emerge in a man? How does a passive or withdrawn man typically respond?

2. Why are the reactions of a woman whose husband is undergoing a crisis so critical? How do the apostle Paul's words in 1 Thessalonians 5:14–15 apply?

3. A withdrawn man is convinced that underneath everything, he is a failure. How can a wife help her husband focus on hope?

4. What is there about your spouse that first attracted you to him or her?

Chapter 6
The Workaholic

1. How can a *passive* husband be a workaholic? To make money and to provide for family are only partial reasons why men work. Name other reasons.

2. A man who overworks because he feels inferior often values quantity over quality. Why is this dangerous?

3. How does a workaholic tend to view the Christian life?

4. How does work or other activities that keep you busy make you feel? If you didn't have to work, how would you spend your time?

Chapter 7
The Escapist

1. Escapists are known by their chronic irresponsibility. Name some other traits.

2. What should a wife avoid doing when dealing with an escapist?

3. Passive resistance—doing nothing—may seem a difficult tack, but how can it impact an escapist's irresponsible tendencies? How does it help stem a wife's growing anger and resentment toward her husband?

4. Are there areas in your life in which you play the part of an escapist? Recurring situations in which you treat your spouse like a grade-schooler?

Chapter 8
A Portrait of the Man David

1. What aspects of David's homelife would naturally diminish a person's self-esteem? David dealt with a great deal of sibling rivalry. What can be done to quell this timeless problem?

2. When a child grows up in a home where he is ignored, what unfortunate lessons is he apt to learn?

3. How can you build up the self-esteem of your child or mate and stop the cycle of criticism?

4. Who were your role models growing up? To whom are you a role model?

Chapter 9
Abigail, the Doormat With Lace

1. Suppressing bitterness and hostility was one sign that Abigail was overly submissive. How can avoiding confrontation affect a marriage? In what other ways was Abigail overly submissive?

2. We often view ourselves according to our own standards or those of our friends and family. Why should self-worth or self-acceptance be based on God?

3. What daily habits are necessary to accept ourselves and guard against being overly submissive?

4. Submission is a Christian virtue, not just a mandate to women. Reflecting on the past few days, have there been situations in which you submitted to another? Was it your choice—a decision to be like Christ—or were there other reasons? What can be learned from the situation(s)?

Chapter 10
The Woman at War

1. The source of chronic anger is internal, not due to outer circumstances or difficult people. What does chronic anger reveal about us? How can it be dealt with?

2. Part of Michal's anger likely came from feeling like a spectator in David's life. Neglect can trigger what other feelings? What guidance does 1 Peter 3:7 offer husbands?

3. In what ways can unresolved conflicts and anger affect a sexual relationship? Why is the sexual union the wrong place to negotiate for recognition?

4. Think back to the last emotional outburst you or your spouse had. Was it due to a hidden "minefield"—an unsettled conflict? What steps can be taken to combat this chronic anger?

Chapter 11
Bathsheba, the Manipulating Woman

1. When a husband abandons his leadership role and becomes distant, his wife may respond with bitter and silent submission or strike back with anger or manipulation. Why is sexual manipulation harmful to both marriage partners?

2. What other strategies do many women use to punish or manipulate their husbands? If change occurs as a result of manipulation, why is it usually short-term?

3. Since manipulation is harmful, how should a wife who's feeling ignored energize her marriage? How can confrontation be used in a positive manner?

4. Marriage is a ministry—an opportunity to make a significant difference in the life of another person. How do you minister to your spouse? How does he or she minister to you? What are your spouse's greatest needs, and how can God use you to supply them?

Chapter 12
The Woman at Work

1. How is a woman's view of marriage and work generally different from a man's outlook? What happens when a husband thinks his primary responsibility is simply to be a good provider?

2. Pressures at home and at work—plus having a distant or weak husband—usually result in a stress-filled life for a woman. What inner attitudes create or intensify this stress? Why is thinking that love must be earned, particularly damaging?

3. What thoughts and actions are helpful for escaping the stress-trap?

4. Husbands: What specific things can you do to shoulder some of the burdens weighing down your wife? Wives: What can *you* do to relieve any responsibility pressures you're feeling? How can your husband and family help?

Chapter 13
Stopping the Cycle in Your Children

1. What roles do love and discipline have in building a boy's confidence so that he can become a strong and sensitive leader? What does a child learn from how we spend our time and money?

2. Why is personal responsibility such an important trait to foster in a child? What are the best approaches for correcting misbehavior and building a child's values?

3. Why is a hurried, competitive life harmful to a child?

4. What characteristic traits, both positive and negative, do you see in your children? What can you and your spouse do to encourage any necessary changes?